Chef Jessica Catalano

The Ganja Kitchen Revolution

The Bible of Cannabis Cuisine

Photography by Tyler Kittock

Green Candy Press

The Ganga Kitchen Revolution
Published by Green Candy Press

Copyright © 2013 Jessica Catalano

ISBN 978-1-937866-92-1
eBook ISBN 978-1-937866-93-8

Photographs © Tyler Kittock
Cover photograph © Thomas Blanchard
Photographs on Page 6 © Green Candy Press
Photographs on Pages 14 and 18 © Jasper Potts

This book contains information about illegal substances, specifically the plant Cannabis Sativa and its derivative products. Green Candy Press would like to emphasize that Cannabis is a controlled substance in North America and throughout much of the world. As such, the use and cultivation of cannabis can carry heavy penalties that may threaten an individual's liberty and livelihood.

The aim of the Publisher is to educate and entertain. Whatever the Publisher's view on the validity of current legislation, we do not in any way condone the use of prohibited substances.

Printed in China by 1010 Printing.

Sometimes Massively Distributed by P.G.W.

Dedication

Cannabis Sativa, Cannabis Indica, and Cannabis Ruderalis:
Thank you for being the "Gateway drug" to perpetual inspiration,
compassion, benevolence, and medicinal miracles.

Contents

Contents

Introduction

The Ganja Kitchen Revolution

The Ganja Kitchen Revolution was born from the coming together of three passions: alternative medicine, healthy cooking and taking care of people in need. I have loved being in the kitchen ever since I can remember. When I was very young, I would beg my parents to let me cook or bake for them, but at the time I was so little that I wasn't allowed to be in the kitchen by myself for fear that I may accidentally get hurt. So instead, I was taught recipes under the wing of my caretakers until I reached the age where I could be in the area unsupervised. Preparing food came so naturally to me that I would actively look for excuses to create dishes for myself or others; I found it immensely pleasurable, relaxing, centering and reenergizing. As I grew up, I was exposed to many different cultural backgrounds of food and my culinary skills improved.

I was first introduced to the fine art of making edibles in early 1997 when I was merely a teenager, and I have been enamored ever since. Of course, back then I did not know as much as I do now. All I knew was that I had stumbled across a powerful herbal medicine that eradicated my painful chronic migraines. I learned classic, simple cannabis culture recipes at first, such as brownies, cakes and cookies, which were very inconspicuous in a non-compassionate state. Throughout my younger years, I experimented with various recipes but was always limited to a minimal strain selection due to the legality situation in Upstate New York.

At 23, I went west and left Buffalo, NY for the majestic mountains of Colorado. While working in the healthcare field before and after my move, I learned a great deal about the detrimental and sometimes devastating effects of manufactured, pharmaceutical drugs. Attending an emergency medical technology program and then doing my clinicals before graduation only made me more acutely aware of how bad these for you manufactured drugs can be. Patients were given one pill to fix a specific problem yet ended up with six side effects that required even more pills to fix them in turn. To me this was absolute madness and I was immensely angered by the fact that doctors did this to people. While treating these patients, I often thought to myself that most of these medical conditions would be alleviated or solved if only they ate a clean, well-balanced diet paired with herbal remedies, supplements, and exercise. This observation was amplified once

I transitioned into working at a detox facility and realized how much pill pushing occurred there.

My move to Colorado brought with it the problem of finding a new doctor to monitor and take care of my migraines. I was buying cannabis on the unregulated market, but my usage was limited due to random drug testing at my workplace. I had to rely on Western medication which led me down the path of over medicating with prescription pills. Essentially, I became a guinea pig being fed medication after medication because my migraines were not responding to any of the usual treatments. I was being prescribed pills that had sudden cardiac arrest, stroke, hardening of the internal organs and even death listed as possible side effects. I did not like the way the pills made me feel, as most produced very strange sensations in my body: heart palpitations, increased respiration, sweating, high blood pressure, dizziness, nausea, anxiety, nervousness, lethargy and feelings of disconnect were all common experiences for me whilst taking those pills. Cannabis edibles did not give me these side effects and I was upset that I couldn't use them as much as I wanted to. Eventually, my time was up in the detox unit as I had been putting myself through Culinary Arts School with the ultimate goal to work in a bakery. When that dream became reality, I found myself in a quaint little bakery in Denver that had been in operation since 1951. After settling in, I was told by a friend at the bakery—much to my surprise— that medical cannabis was legal in Colorado and that I should look into it since the bakery did not do random drug tests. That night I researched the laws surrounding medical cannabis and made an appointment with a medical

cannabis doctor the next day. After the long process of medical record checking, questions, conversations and paperwork, I was granted my temporary medical cannabis paper license until my red card came in the mail.

I was allowed to purchase my medication on the same visit and I was absolutely floored the moment I stepped into the medication room; an intoxicating aroma of freshly cured buds laced the air and smelled so sweet you could almost taste it. Big glass jars full of fluffy organic buds lined the shelves on the back wall while tinctures, edibles, and lotions were displayed in a large glass case. The man who was behind the counter—known as a budtender —picked out specific strains that would help combat my migraines. Because it was my first time, he explained the basic principles of the genetic makeup of the plants and how it would affect me. I was becoming overwhelmed because I never would have experienced something like this back home and I wasn't sure how to handle it. My unease then transitioned to thoughts of cops waiting outside in the parking lot for me in some sort of sting operation. As these worries began to flood my mind, I realized I was experiencing a bit of a culture shock. I told myself to relax before I gave myself an anxiety attack and calmed myself with pranayama breathing.

Crisis averted, I bought my first strain of legal weed, Island Sweet Skunk, along with a vaporizer. Each time I went to the dispensary to pick up my medication I would learn more and more about the different strains. I spent excessive amounts of time talking to the budtenders, owners, and doctors, forever picking their brains to learn as much as I could. I was also captivated by all the different flavors

Introduction

and smell profiles of the strains I bought or saw in the dispensary. This fascination led me to experiment with recipes in which the strains would actually make the dishes taste better and enhance their flavors. Going to Culinary Arts School as a double major and my desire to live a healthy lifestyle led me to take edibles to the next level. As my tastes developed, I found that while brownies and other classic cannabis treats were fun to eat in high school, I wanted healthier food items that would heal my body and act as a delicious vessel for the medicinal benefits of cannabis. I truly believe that you need to be conscious of the fact that food is a medicine in itself, and that dishes should not only be elegant and delicious but deliver powerful health benefits as well. Thus, the Ganja Kitchen Revolution was born. It is about taking nutrient-rich dishes and adding strain-specific medical cannabis for medicinal effects and specific flavors, so that each dish becomes the best well-rounded gift I can give to a patient in need of therapeutic alternative medicine.

In this book, I have designed recipes that will taste gourmet but without the worry of fancy knife skills, expensive kitchen equipment or overly complicated recipes. I created these recipes so that anyone could cook them with confidence, despite a lack of experience, time or physical ability to slave over a stove. I have also incorporated my love for international cuisine due to my exposure to different food cultures growing up. I believe that food (and life) should be experienced to the fullest, and enjoying international recipes is one of the best ways to do this at home.

Two of the most important lessons to be learned from this book are how to properly dose your medication and how to use strains that actually enhance the flavors of your dishes. One of my biggest pet peeves is carelessly dosed edibles that have been made with overcooked butter, so bitter and highly dosed it would be enough to permanently scare someone away from edibles for life. Through the chapters of this book, you will grasp the concepts of how to dose each serving of a dish so that you will not over or under medicate yourself. The revolutionary dosing chart contained in this book is in half-gram increments, starting at ¼ gram and going all the way to 2½ grams, which will make dosing your dishes much easier. This chart will outline which gram dosage provides the best alleviation of symptoms for various medical conditions . By using this in conjunction with the different recipes in the book, you can create a foolproof method to medicate the right way. The strain and alternative strain chart will also explain what flavors the cannabis imparts to each dish. The flavor profiles of these strains can interact with the aromas of the cannabis, thus creating a pleasant sensory experience in more ways than one!

Finally, it is my opinion that cannabis food is the most natural, healthiest and effective way to medicate. When cannabis is ingested in the form of food, your body processes the Tetrahydrocannabinol (THC) in your liver into the psychoactive metabolite 11-Hydroxy-THC. This metabolite creates a stronger, longer-lasting and more full-body effect compared to the effects of smoked or vaporized THC. Not to mention that there are over 100 different cannabinoids (that scientists know of) that have been isolated from the cannabis plant. These cannabinoids play a role in supporting different functions of THC as well as the functions in your body. Our bodies are actually designed to process THC, 11-Hydroxy-THC and the different cannabinoids because they are equipped with cannabinoid receptors. You can never overdose or die from Cannabis, nor does it cause devastating side effects that are detrimental to your health like pharmaceutical drugs. It is by far the safest alternative medicine. Viva la good health!

Strain Flavor Profiles and Alternative Strains

The chart below is designed to outline the flavor profiles of each of the strains used in this book. In each recipe, I have used a strain that not only compliments but actually enhances the flavors of the dish itself. These are all strains that are common in the Colorado area. However, The Ganja Kitchen Revolution is a world-wide phenomenon, and in your area, it might not be so easy to lay your hands on some Blue Pearl or Yumboldt. With this in mind, I've created an alternative strain chart to allow you to substitute each recipe's original strain with one that's more available to you. Every strain has several alternatives listed, but you can also substitute with any strain or kief of your choice that has a similar flavor profile and genetic makeup.

Strain or Kief	Genetic Makeup	Flavor Profile	Alternative Strains or Kief
HeadBand	**Indica Dominant Hybrid** 70% Indica 30% Sativa	Earthy with strong notes of pine and diesel	Death Star, OG HeadBand, Moolah, Burmese Kush and K.O Kush
Silver Haze	**True Hybrid** 50% Sativa 50% Indica	Fruity pine with menthol undertones	Arjan's Haze #1, Buddha Haze, Super Skunk, Hawaiian Big Bud and Northern Lights x Skunk
Caramella	**Indica Dominant Hybrid** 80% Indica 20% Sativa	Sweet with caramel and candy tones	Vanilluna, Cotton Candy x Romulan, Cream Caramel and Orange Kush x Ice Cream
Lavender	**Indica Dominant Hybrid** 80% Indica 20% Sativa	Hash with undertones of lavender and spice	Hash Dawg, Hash Plant, Hash Heaven and Magic Bud
Elvis	**Hybrid** Unknown Genetic Percentage	Sandalwood with hash, floral, berry, skunk and spice notes	Perma Frost, White Russian, Maui Wowie and Hash Plant

Strains

Strain or Kief	Genetic Makeup	Flavor Profile	Alternative Strains or Kief
Strawberry Haze	**Sativa Dominant Hybrid** 70% Sativa 30% Indica	Sweet strawberry with hints of rose petals	Strawberry Cough, Strawberry Ice and Strawberry Kush
NYC Diesel	**Sativa Dominant Hybrid** 60% Sativa 40% Indica	Tart with diesel, lemon and heavy citrus tones	Dutch Treat, Diesel, Chiesel, Golden Goat and New York Power Diesel
Diabolic Funxta	**Sativa Dominant Hybrid** 70% Sativa 30% Indica	Diesel with heavy floral and citrus notes	Dutch Treat, Diesel, Chiesel and New York Power Diesel
Haze	**100% Sativa**	Pine with prominent skunk and earth tones	Ivory Haze, Super Silver Haze, Silver Haze and Purple Haze
Exodus Cheese	**Indica Dominant Hybrid** 60% Indica 40% Sativa	Cheese with earthy undertones	Big Cheese, Sweet Cheese, Cheese, Platinum Cheese and Big Buddha Cheese
Blue Pearl	**Sativa Dominant Hybrid** 70% Sativa 30% Indica	Lemon with refreshing citrus tones	Lemon Skunk, Lemon Lime Kush and Lemonberry
Mako Haze	**Sativa Dominant Hybrid** 75% Sativa 25% Indica	Earth with notes of sandalwood and spice	Hash Plant, Shoreline, Purple Haze and Spice
Mandala #1	**Hybrid** Unknown Genetic Percentage	Citrus with smoke and earth undertones	White Rhino, LSD, Blockhead, Querkle and Purple Passion
Mekong High	**Sativa Dominant Hybrid** 75% Sativa 25% Indica	Spicy with heavy earth and pepper tones	Hash Plant, Spice, Shoreline and Trainwreck #2
Sour Diesel	**Sativa Dominant Hybrid** 90% Sativa 10% Indica	Diesel with heavy sourness, lemon, pine and earth	Sour Diesel #2, Sour Kush, Sour OG and Sour Diesel IBL
B-52	**Indica Dominant Hybrid** 75% Indica 25% Sativa	Sweet pine with skunk and lemon notes	Sweet Island Skunk, Lemon Skunk, Golden Goat and Headcheese
The Third Dimension	**Sativa Dominant Hybrid** 70% Sativa 30% Indica	Tart tropical fruit with lemon tones	Sweet Island Skunk, Lemon Skunk, Blue Dream, Caribbean Dream and Dutch Treat
Yumboldt	**100% Indica**	Pine with skunky undertones	Master Kush, OG Kush and Tangerine Kush. You can also substitute with any strain or kief of your choice that has a similar flavor profile and genetic makeup

Strains

Strain or Kief	Genetic Makeup	Flavor Profile	Alternative Strains or Kief
Cheesus	**Indica Dominant Hybrid** 60% Indica 40% Sativa	Sweet earth with pine, spice, tartness, fruit and slight cheese undertones	Cheesewreck, Headcheese, Cheesel, Cheese and Sweet Cheese
Speed Queen	**Indica Dominant Hybrid** Unknown Genetic Percentage	Fruity citrus with floral, mint and skunk tones	Fruit of the Gods, Belladonna, Blush and Blue Mistic
Blue Cheese	**Indica Dominant Hybrid** 80% Indica 20% Sativa	Cheese with undertones of sweet fruit, musk and spice	Exodus Cheese, Big Cheese, Sweet Cheese, Cheese, Platinum Cheese and Big Buddha Cheese
Lemon Kush	**Indica Dominant Hybrid** Unknown Genetic Percentage	Lemon with floral and peppermint notes	Lemon Lime Kush, Blue Pearl, Lemon Skunk, Lemonberry and Super Lemon Haze
Afghan Kush	**100% Indica**	Citrus with sweet, fruit, musk and mild skunk undertones	Grace Slick, Lil Afghani, Afghani #1, Pure Afghan and Afghani
Super Lemon Haze	**Sativa Dominant Hybrid** Unknown Genetic Percentage	Candied lemon with sweet floral notes	Lemon Lime Kush, Blue Pearl, Lemon Skunk, Lemonberry and Super Lemon Haze
Carnival	**Sativa Dominant Hybrid** 80% Sativa 20% Indica	Sugary lemon with hints of mixed citrus	Blue Pearl, Lemon Skunk, Dutch Treat, Ice and Super Lemon Haze
Skunk #1	**Sativa Dominant Hybrid** Unknown Genetic Percentage	Light Skunk with sweet minimal hash and fruit undertones	Blue Dream, Skunk #9, Skunk Haze and Super Skunk
Spice	**True Hybrid** 50% Sativa 50% Indica	Hash with sandalwood and exotic fruit like undertones	Hash Plant, Hash Heaven, Hash Master and Hashberry
Lemon Skunk	**Sativa Dominant Hybrid** 60% Sativa 40% Indica	Citrus with bold skunk and fruit notes	Lemon Lime Kush, Blue Pearl, Lemonberry and Super Lemon Haze
Hash Plant	**100% Indica**	Heavy earth notes mixed with hash	Black Domina, Hash Plant, Hash Heaven and Hash Master. You can also substitute with any strain or kief of your choice that has a similar flavor profile and genetic makeup
Shiva	**Indica Dominant Hybrid** Unknown Genetic Percentage	Sweet skunk with earthy pine tones	Jack Kevorkian, Satori, Urban Poison and Shiva Skunk
ChemDawg D	**Indica Dominant Hybrid** Unknown Genetic Percentage	Pine with skunky earth tones	Northern Lights, Northern Lights #1, Northern Lights x Skunk and Nice Guy

Strains

Strain or Kief	Genetic Makeup	Flavor Profile	Alternative Strains or Kief
Banana Kush	**Indica Dominant Hybrid** 60% Indica 40% Sativa	Banana with sweet fruity undertones	Banana, Juicy Fruit, Blue Banana and Banana Diesel
Mango	**100% Indica**	Mango with sweet fruity undertones	Papaya, Hollands Hope and Shishkaberry
DJ Short's Blueberry	**Indica Dominant Hybrid** 60% Indica 40% Sativa	Blueberry with sugar and minimal spice notes	Blueberry, Blue God, Blue Dynamite, Blackberry Kush and Chem Berry
Ultra Skunk	**Sativa Dominant Hybrid** Unknown Genetic Percentage	Fruit with sweet skunk and floral notes	Caribbean Dream, Juicy Skunk and Lime Green Skunk
Strawberry Cough	**Sativa Dominant Hybrid** 80% Sativa 20% Indica	Strawberry with sugar and cream	Strawberry Skunk, Chem Crème, Purple Strawberry Kush and Strawberry Haze
Pineapple Kush	**100% Indica**	Pineapple with sweet yet tart fruity undertones	Pineapple Afghan, Brazilian Amazonian, God Bud, Buddha's Sister and Reclining Buddha
Orange Kush	**Indica Dominant Hybrid** 80% Indica 20% Sativa	Orange with sweet citrus floral notes	Orange Crush, Cali Orange, Agent Orange and Orange Velvet
Shiva Skunk	**Indica Dominant Hybrid** Unknown Genetic Percentage	Spice with strong skunk notes with sweet undertones	Shiva, Jack Kevorkian, Satori, Urban Poison and Hindu Kush
Super Nova	**Indica Dominant Hybrid** Unknown Genetic Percentage	Strong pine notes with a slight bitter taste	Northern Lights, Northern Lights #1, Northern Lights x Skunk and Super Skunk
Conquistador	**Indica Dominant Hybrid** Unknown Genetic Percentage	Sweet citrus with melon undertones	Blue Velvet, True Blue, Blue Dragon, 8 Miles High and Juicy Skunk
Herijuana	**Indica Dominant Hybrid** 80% Indica 20% Sativa	Hash with sandalwood and dark roast coffee notes	Night Train, Lowryder #2, Psicodelicia. Himalaya Gold andGreen- O -Matic
Wappa	**100% Indica**	Earth with pungent fruit mixed with musk	Maple Leaf Indica, Ortega Indica, California Indica and Tora Bora
Somativa	**Indica Dominant Hybrid** 60% Indica 40% Sativa	Sweet skunk mixed with floral pine	Northern Lights x Skunk, Satori, Wonder Woman and Widow Skunk
Chrystal	**Indica Dominant Hybrid** 60% Indica 40% Sativa	Kerosene with heavy citrus notes	Sensi Star, Tangerine Dream, The Church, Hawaii x Maui Waui and Special K

Strains

Strain or Kief	Genetic Makeup	Flavor Profile	Alternative Strains or Kief
Sputnik	**Sativa Dominant Hybrid** 70% Sativa 30% Indica	Cream with slight sour undertones	Dairy Queen, X-Dog, Swiss Cheese, Cheese and Snow White
Red Devil	**100% Indica**	Floral with heavy forest aromatics	Northern Lights, Northern Lights #1, Purple Kush, The Teenone and Ivory Haze
Mazar	**Indica Dominant Hybrid** 80% Indica 20% Sativa	Strong sandalwood and pine notes	Hash Plant, Kushage, Millennium, S.A.G.E, Sadhu and Shaman
Kalichakra	**Sativa Dominant Hybrid** Unknown Genetic Percentage	Sweet with a fruity mint undertone	Hawaiian Snow, Frisian Dew, A.M.S, Pamir Gold and Double Fun
Berry Kush	**Indica Dominant Hybrid** Unknown Genetic Percentage	Blueberry with sweet berry undertones	Blackberry Kush, Master x Blackberry, Juicy Fruit, Incrediberry and Fruity Pebbles
Chocolope	**Sativa Dominant Hybrid** 5% Sativa 5% Indica	Chocolate with sweet fruit and smoky notes	Thai-Tanic, Thai Stick, Chocolate Rain and Dj Short Cocoa Kush
Somalicious	**100% Indica**	Heavy hash with sweet notes	Black Domina, Afghani, Sweet Afghani Delicious S1 and Durga Mata
Nebula	**Indica Dominant Hybrid** 80% Indica 20% Sativa	Sweet with a strong skunk tang and subtle earthiness	Love Cheese, Critical Jack, Snowbud, Oasis and Buddha Haze
Chocolate Thai	**100% Sativa**	Chocolate with a rich full bodied coffee taste	Alaskan Thunder Fuck, Chocolope Haze, Chocolate Chip Cookies, Sativa Chocolate Chip and Chocolope
Ice Cream	**Indica Dominant Hybrid** 60% Indica 40% Sativa	Sugary with strong vanilla tones	Cotton Candy, Sugar Babe, Vanilla Haze, Vanilluna and Magic Bud
Romulan	**100% Indica**	Pungent sweet and spicy tones	Northern Lights, Northern Lights #1, Romulan x Hash Plant, Grape Romulan and Romulan x UK Cheese x Afghani
Vanilla Kush	**100% Indica**	Creamy vanilla with subtle floral undertones	Cotton Candy Kush
ABV (Already Been Vaped)	**Indica, Sativa, Indica Dominant Hybrid, Sativa Dominant Hybrid or True Hybrid**	Lightly sweet like corn syrup with very mild floral tones	N/A

Strains

Author's notes

In the above chart, you'll find the genetic makeup for every strain in this book. This is so that if you choose your own alternative strain, you can help look for ones that might give similar effects. All hybrids regardless of Indica or Sativa dominancy can be substituted for any other kind of hybrid genetics. For example, you can substitute the strain Ice Cream, which is an Indica dominant hybrid (60/40), with the true hybrid Vanilluna (50/50). This is perfectly fine to do since they both fall under the umbrella "Hybrid" category. ABV Cannabis does not have a burnt popcorn taste or smell when properly vaporized. It should be lightly sweet and floral in taste when prepared in food.

Flavor Profile

The flavor profile explains what flavors the cannabis or kief imparts to each dish. The primary flavors are sweet, sour, salty, bitter and savory which combine to create a "flavor profile." This flavor profile can be further related with the aromas of the cannabis thus creating a pleasant sensory experience. As a side note, any "salty" tasting cannabis is usually a direct result of using chemical flushes or chemicals during the growing process.

Revolutionary Dosing Chart

An Easy Guide to Medicate

.25 grams	.50 grams	.75 grams	1.0 gram	1.25 grams	1.50 grams	1.75 grams	2.0 grams	2.25 grams
½ teaspoon	1 tsp	1½ tsp	2 tsps	2½ tsps	3 tsps	3½ tsps	4 tsps	4½ tsps

This revolutionary dosing chart is in half-gram increments starting at .25 grams and going all the way to 2.5 grams. Each gram increment is also broken down into teaspoon measurements. Finally, you do not have to worry about fancy scales and you can dose your medical cannabis with the most common household item, the teaspoon. The dosing chart will outline which medical conditions fall under the specific gram dosage for the best alleviation of symptoms. This chart used in conjunction with the different recipes within the book creates a foolproof way for you as a medical cannabis patient to medicate the right way, and be consistent each time. Finally, you will be able to know what the best dose is for your medical needs and create dishes that deliver the same amount of medicine in each serving.

You no longer have to worry about second guessing how much medical cannabis is in each serving, or worry that you might over or under medicate yourself. With this chart you will be able to be 100% confident that each serving of medical cannabis in your dish will be the same in each serving. To find the perfect dose of medical cannabis for your medical needs: start with the smallest dose on this chart first, and then work your way up if you feel you need more relief for your medical condition until you find the right dose that works the best for you. As you do this, try one dose to see how it works for you and then wait at least 8 hours before you try the next dose, if the first does not alleviate your medical condition. 8 hours gives you ample time to figure out if the selected dose works or not and how your body responds

to it. This time frame will also allow a big enough window to see how long the medicinal effects of the dose you chose will last in your system. You will be able to make an informed decision on how well a dose works or doesn't work for you. Keep doing this until you find the right dose for your medical condition. It will usually take about 1 hour for the effects of medical cannabis to process in your body, but some patients may be able to feel the effects in as little as 30 minutes. It all depends on how fast your body can metabolize the Tetrahydrocannabinol mixed with the dish that you consumed.

Remember, the conditions contained within this chart are based on the most common treatable medical conditions outlined by medical cannabis friendly states. If you have a condition that is not

Dosing

Conditions That Can Benefit From Cannabis

Migraines

Insomnia

Loss of appetite

Inflammation

Arthritis

ADD

ADHD

Glaucoma

Menstrual Cramps

PTSD

Muscle pain, Joint pain

Neuropathic pain

Depression and anxiety

Cancer

HIV/AIDS

Multiple Sclerosis

Fibromyalgia

Gastrointestinal disorders

Cluster Headaches

Muscle Spasms

Anorexia

Epilepsy

Nausea

Pain

Spasticity

AIDS Wasting Syndrome

Parkinson's disease

Rheumatoid Arthritis

Accidents and injuries

Irritable bowel syndrome IBS

Crohn's disease

Cachexia

Tremors and seizures

mentioned in this chart, don't fret; it's more than likely that medical cannabis will benefit from the use of the dishes within this book. The best thing is to check with a doctor to discuss the effects that medical cannabis may have on your condition and discuss whether it's right for you. The same goes for conditions that are already outlined in the chart: it's always a good idea to talk with your medical provider before you start any alternative medicine or treatment. Another note to keep in mind in case you try a dose and you find out it is too much for you; you cannot overdose and die from ingesting medical cannabis no matter what. So if you find you have tried a dose that seems to be too much, the best thing to do is have a cup of fruit juice or some other kind of natural sugar that will raise your blood sugar slightly and lie down to relax until it passes.

* 1.25 grams, 1.50 grams, 1.75 grams, 2.0 grams and 2.25 grams are considered the heavier doses. While these higher doses can treat the same medical conditions as the lower doses, these higher doses are for the severe end of the medical condition spectrum. Heavier doses like these should only be consumed once your body has gotten used to the effects of medical cannabis versus just consuming 2.0 grams right off the bat. Start with the smallest dose on this chart first and then work your way up

if you feel you need more relief for your medical condition until you find the right dose that works the best for you.

** The gram increments in this dosing chart are for ground bud and for kief. If the recipe calls for decarboxylized bud or kief, follow the decarboxylation process below.

To properly decarboxylize cured buds

Preheat your oven to 220°F. Take a baking sheet and lay your ground up medical cannabis buds onto the sheet and make sure that it is evenly disbursed. Place the baking sheet into the oven uncovered and heat for 25 minutes. Pull the baking sheet from the oven and let it cool completely. You now have decarboxylized or activated medical cannabis that is ready for consumption. When you place this decarboxylized weed into recipes, it will "activate" further between the heat of the cooking process and any lipid content contained within the recipe.

To properly decarboxylize kief

Preheat your oven to 220°F. Take a baking sheet and very carefully sprinkle the kief onto the sheet and make sure that it is evenly disbursed. Place the baking sheet into the oven uncovered and heat for 25 minutes. Pull the baking sheet from the oven and let it cool

Dosing

completely. The kief will become sticky so be very careful when removing it from the pan. You now have decarboxylized or "activated" medical kief that is ready for consumption. When you place this decarboxylized kief into recipes, it will activate further between the heat of the cooking process and any lipid content contained within the recipe.

To ensure proper and even dosing

It is highly recommended that you use a simple kitchen scale with each recipe in this book to weigh the final product for some cooked items, and to weigh the proportions of certain baked items beforehand. Some items such as basic cannabutter, oils, extract, nut butters, drinks, raw food items, and cakes are exempt from this process. Using a kitchen scale to divide the portions equally will ensure a proper and even dose per serving. For example, you can take a large bowl and add the final product of Hungarian Wappa Goulash on the scale for the total weight. Then divide the total weight of the product into 4 servings which is what the recipe will yield. For the American Chewy Vegan Chocolate Thai Kief Chip Cookies recipe, you should weigh the dough evenly before baking them. The following lists outline which recipes you need to weigh either before or after and which ones are exempt from this process.

Recipes to be weighed before baking/cooking

Americana Elvis Pancakes

English Lavender Buttermilk Current Scones

American Blue Pearl Ahi Tuna Sandwich (weighing the sauce)

American Yumboldt Chicken Club Sandwich (weighing the guacamole)

American Herbed Blue Cheese Biscuits

American ABV Strawberry Shortcake

American Chewy Vegan Chocolate Thai Kief Chip Cookies

German Vanilla Kush Marzipan

Japanese Green Tea Mochi Ice Cream

The American Romulan Ho Ho Cupcake

Recipes to be weighed after baking/cooking

Bajan Silver Haze Sweet Bread

Italian Diabolic Funxta Eggs in Purgatory

Italian Exodus Cheese Frittata

Jewish American Caramella Coffee Cake

Venezuelan Haze Scrambled Eggs

Warm Honey HeadBand Kief Walnuts in Greek Yogurt

Chinese Chicken Mekong High Lettuce Cups

Indian Mandala #1 Curried Chickpeas

Lebanese Sour Diesel Taboull

Thai Mako Haze Kief Beef Salad

Algerian Skunk # 1 Salad

Central Italian Lemon Skunk Bruschetta

East African Spice Pea Soup

French ABV Brie En Croûte

Middle Eastern Afghan Kush Hummus

Super Lemon Haze Mexican Guacamole

American Tex-Mex Herijuana Cinnamon Chili

German Super Nova Meatloaf

Hungarian Wappa Goulash

Indian Shiva Skunk Chicken Curry

Italian Eggplant in Red Devil Sauce

Moroccan Mazar Lamb

Russian Sputnik Beef Stroganoff

Sicilian Somativa Veal Marsala

American Chocolope Frosted Raw Brownies

American Somalicious Kief Applesauce

Egyptian Nebula Semolina Cake

French Mixed Berry Kush Compote

Kalichakra Indian Sweet Carrot Pudding

Recipes to be exempt

Jewish American NYC Diesel Lox Bagel

Strawberry Haze French Toast

Basic Clarified Cannabutter

Basic Clarified Herbed Cannabutter

Basic Compound Strawberry Honey Cannabutter

Basic Madagascar Vanilla Bean Bourbon Extract

Basic Olive Oil

Basic Raw Coconut Honey

Basic Raw Coconut Oil

Lightly Medicated Basic Hazelnut Butter

Lightly Medicated Basic Honey Peanut Butter

Rosemary Marjoram Infused Oil

list continues ...

Dosing

Dietary Lifestyles

Being aware of dietary lifestyle choices is important as they cater to the health issues, religious practices, political stances, environmental concerns, and the beliefs and values of others. I've included the 7 most common groups of dietary lifestyles in today's society: omnivore, ovo-lacto-vegetarian, ovo-vegetarian, lacto-vegetarian, demi-vegetarian, vegan and gluten free.

DIETARY LIFESTYLE CHART	
Key	**Meaning**
O	Omnivore
OLV	Ovo-lacto-vegetarian a.k.a Vegetarian
OV	Ovo-vegetarian
LV	Lacto-vegetarian
P	Pescetarian
V	Vegan
GF	Gluten free

Omnivores rank as the predominant dietary lifestyle choice and have an easier time with food choices as they can eat anything without restrictions. Ovo-lacto-vegetarians are also known by the blanket term "vegetarian." This is the most popular alternative diet as you can consume plant, dairy and egg products. Ovo-vegetarian typically is a vegetarian who eats eggs but does not consume dairy products. On the reverse side is the lacto-vegetarian, who is a vegetarian who will consume dairy products but will not eat eggs. Pescetarians are ovo-lacto-vegetarians who include the consumption of fish in their diet. Vegans do not consume any animal meat whatsoever or any products derived from living or dead animals. The gluten-free lifestyle is for people who either medically cannot or who choose not to consume any foods containing gluten.

The dietary lifestyle chart is designed as a key to all of the recipes contained within this book. Each letter or key represents a dietary lifestyle choice and will help you to pick recipes out of this book that fit your dietary need. Remember; do not feel trapped by this chart. It is merely a guideline for recipes that fit your dietary lifestyle which can be prepared as written in the book. The reality is any recipe in this book can be fit into your dietary lifestyle choice if you choose to make the necessary adjustments. For example, if you are vegan and a recipe calls for honey but every other ingredient in that recipe is vegan, then the recipe will not be labeled vegan. However, if you want to make this recipe vegan, simply substitute the honey for something like agave nectar and then you will have a recipe that is 100% vegan. So really, anyone can use any recipe in this book so long as you are aware of what items need to be substituted.

Getting the Basics Right: Cannabutter and Oil

The process of ingesting medical cannabis to relieve the symptoms of your medical condition really is the most natural, most healthy and most effective way to ingest cannabis. Not only that, but when you ingest cannabis, the body breaks the THC into the psychoactive metabolite 11-Hydroxy-THC, which creates a stronger, longer-lasting and a more full-body effect compared to the effects of smoked or vaporized medical cannabis. This effect, paired with other cannabinoids, is ideal for treating medical conditions which require the management of symptoms over a longer period of time and require a strong medicine.

Vaporized medical cannabis is the next best thing to eating edibles as the psychoactive ingredients are evaporated without causing the irritating effects of combustion. Yet even with vaporization, you are still possibly inhaling minute particles in the form of vapors and you run the risk of accidently combusting the medical cannabis if you do not know how to properly use a vaporizer. Smoking, while nostalgic to most people, is really the worst way to consume medical cannabis. Like all smoke, cannabis smoke creates carcinogens which, in the long run, can adversely affect your health or increase the risk of respiratory infections regardless of the THC and cannabinoids contained within the smoke. Sure, smoking cannabis is not as detrimental to your health as smoking a cigarette, but even still, smoke is smoke.

Medical cannabis needs to be activated through heat, fat or alcohol. THC is hydrophobic, which means it is insoluble in water but soluble in lipids or alcohol. Because of the hydrophobic nature of THC, it can be extracted to any fat or alcohol of the patients' choice. Heat activates the medical cannabis through the process of decarboxylation. During this heating process a reaction occurs within the carboxylic acid in the cannabis, which results in the psychoactive properties of THC. All three processes also prepare the cannabinoids found within the cannabis for entry into the patient's body, where it can be further metabolised in the liver.

Once you have determined your method of activation, you'll need to choose your dose based on the revolutionary dosing chart in Chapter 3. You will find that this chart is in half-gram increments starting at .25 grams

and going all the way to 2.5 grams. Each gram increment is also broken down into teaspoon measurements to make dosing your medical cannabis easy and worry-free. I recommend that everyone start at the lowest dose of .25 grams and then work their way up to the other doses if need be. You should be able to easily find the perfect dose that works for you in the chart. Based on this chart, you will be able to create proper and uniform dosed cannabutter and oils. This

means is that with each serving you will consume the same dose of medical cannabis, eliminating concerns about over or under medicating. For example, if you choose to make Basic Clarified Cannabutter with .25 grams for your first time, you will add 32 servings of ground cannabis of your choice to 1 pound of butter. After the cooking process on the stove is done, the end result will be 32 servings, or 1 tablespoon per serving, at .25 grams of cannabis each.

During the different activation processes, terpenes in the cannabis, which are responsible for smell and taste, impart their distinct aroma and flavor profiles into whichever dish you choose. The complex flavors of the terpenes can be divided into primary or umbrella flavors of sweet, sour, salty, bitter and savory. With the help of the Strain and Alternative Stain Chart, you will be guided into the art of using certain strains to enhance the smell and flavors of the dishes you create. When

Before You Start

properly cooked, cannabis can impart so many different flavor profiles to dishes that make the consumption of medicated food an overall pleasurable sensory experience. The flavor profiles of cannabis should no longer be ignored but instead embraced by patients.

Two important things regarding the different variations of cannabutter and oil need to be addressed before you delve into your journey of cannabis cooking and baking. The first is the proper color of cannabutter; some people believe "the greener, the better." Unfortunately, having nuclear green cannabutter does not denote a "stronger" cannabutter with a higher "potency" like most patients are led to believe. What it really means is that the butter has been cooked for a period of 6 hours to 24 hours, which in turn releases large amounts of chlorophyll into the butter as the cannabis breaks down. The color has nothing to do with how potent your cannabutter is; rather, it is a clear indication that it has been cooked too long. When cannabis is over cooked like this, the breakdown of chlorophyll causes an extremely bitter and unpleasant taste. This taste is the most common reason that patients turn away from cooking with cannabis. Most of the time when patients complain about their edibles tasting too much like cannabis, or about a brownie tasting too bitter and strong, it is because they are consuming over-cooked cannabutter or oil. In order to avoid this, you simply need to keep the cooking time of cannabutter and oil down to 1 hour. This allows for the proper extraction of THC and other cannabinoids allowing the flavors and aromas of the bud you are using to infuse without becoming overtly bitter and acrid smelling. The result of cooking the cannabutter this way is a creamy, light yellow butter with a slight green hue. For the oils, the result of this cooking will produce a deep golden color with a minor green hue, for olive oil and a creamy white color for coconut oil with a light green hue.

The final important thing to remember when making cannabutter and oils is to only make them with cured buds. Shake, trim and sugar leaves should only be used to create bubble hash or cannabis infused body oils or lotions. The cannabis buds are where the heaviest concentrations of THC, cannabinoids and terpenes lie. Think of it this way: would you make an apple pie with the sticks and leaves from an apple tree and be willing to call it an apple pie? While I understand that many patients want to use every part of the plant in cooking applications, each part of the plant has its own place to be used in these applications. Cannabis buds need to be reserved for cooking, baking, butters, oils, and extracts to ensure that each dish you create is maximized with the largest amount of THC, cannabinoids and terpenes. Therefore, the dosing chart, strain and alternative stain chart, as well as all the recipes contained within this book are based on the usage of cannabis bud. The journey of learning to cook or bake edibles is a pleasurable and deeply knowledgeable experience. If you are a novice at cooking, you need to know you are going to have your ups and downs for any recipe you create whether medicated or not. The most important thing is to remain dedicated to this art and keep practicing the different skills that each dish in this book teaches you. If you are an intermediate cook, this will be a great book to further develop and hone the skills you have already acquired so you can apply them to different situations. As an expert, you will be able to add in precision knife skills along with the ability to add or subtract other components to the recipes based on all the experience you already possess. Whatever your path or level in cannabis cooking may be, there is one rule to live by that will make all the difference in the world. This is something my grandmother always told me to remember and something that, I think, totally sums up the art of cannabis cuisine: "always cook with love."

Butters, Oils & Extracts

Basic Clarified Cannabutter

Directions

Determine your strain and proper dose of cannabis by referring to the dosing chart then set the bud aside in a bowl. On the stove, place the butter in a pan and turn the stove top on to the lowest setting. Allow the butter to melt then add in your ground cannabis strain and dosage of choice. Let this mixture infuse on the stove for 1 hour and stir every so often during this time. Be sure to skim the foam that will form at the top of the butter throughout the cooking process.

After the hour is over, separate the ground cannabis from the cannabutter by running it through a fine mesh strainer or cheesecloth into a bowl. This will separate the milk solids from your cannabutter. Pour your Basic Clarified Cannabutter into a glass jar, ramekin or container of your choice and let it cool for 1 hour in the fridge. During this time the cannabutter will solidify and will be ready for use. Place your Basic Clarified Cannabutter in the fridge for up to 3 months or in the freezer for up to 9 months.

Product Yield

This recipe for Basic Clarified Cannabutter produces 2 cups with 32 servings at 1 tablespoon per serving. Dose strength per tablespoon will be determined by what you choose from the dosing chart.

Mise en place

32 servings of dosed and ground
strain of your choice*
4 sticks or 1 pound of unsalted
sweet cream butter

* Add the suggested amount of ground cannabis or alternative strain of ground cannabis of your choice by referring to the dosing chart on page 15 then the strain and alternative strains chart on page 7

Dietary Lifestyle

O, OLV, LV, P, GF

Clarified Herbed Cannabutter

Mise en place

32 servings of dosed and ground
    strain of your choice*
4 sticks or 1 pound of unsalted
    sweet cream butter
Dried or fresh herbs and/or spices
    of your choice

Directions

Determine your strain and proper dose of cannabis by referring to the dosing chart then set your bud aside in a bowl. On the stove, place the butter in a pan and turn the stove top on to the lowest setting. Allow the butter to melt then add in your ground cannabis strain. Let this mixture infuse on the stove for 1 hour and stir the mixture every so often during this time. Be sure to skim the foam that will form at the top of the butter throughout the cooking process.

After the 1 hour time frame is over, separate the ground cannabis from the cannabutter by running it through a fine mesh strainer or cheesecloth into a bowl. This will separate the milk solids from your cannabutter. Pour your cannabutter into a glass jar, ramekin or container of your choice and let it cool for 1 hour in the fridge. During this time the cannabutter will solidify and will be ready for use.

Remove the Basic Clarified Cannabutter from the fridge and set out at room temperature until softened. You want to use 2 tablespoons of dried or fresh herbs and/or spices per stick as a general guideline. This would mean for 1 pound of basic clarified cannabutter use 8 tablespoons of dried or fresh herbs and/or spices. Add your desired combination of herbs and/or spices into the Basic Clarified Cannabutter then mix until fully incorporated. Place your Basic Clarified Herbed Cannabutter in the fridge for up to 3 months or in the freezer for up to 9 months.

Product Yield

This recipe for Clarified Herbed Cannabutter produces 2 cups with 32 servings at 1 tablespoon each. Dose strength per tablespoon will be determined by what you choose from the dosing chart.

* Add the suggested amount of ground cannabis or alternative strain of ground cannabis of your choice by referring to the dosing chart on page 15 then the strain and alternative strains chart on page 7.

Dietary Lifestyle

O, OLV, LV, P, GF

Compound Strawberry Honey Cannabutter

Directions

Determine your strain and proper dose of cannabis by referring to the dosing chart then set your bud aside in a bowl. On the stove, place the butter in a pan and turn the stovetop on to the lowest setting. Allow the butter to melt then add in your ground cannabis strain. Let this mixture infuse on the stove for 1 hour and stir every so often during this time. Be sure to skim the foam that will form at the top of the butter throughout the cooking process.

* Add the suggested amount of ground cannabis or alternative strain of ground cannabis of your choice by referring to the dosing chart on page 15 then the strain and alternative strains chart on page 7.

Dietary Lifestyle
O, OLV, LV, P, GF

After the hour is over, separate the ground cannabis from the cannabutter by running it through a fine mesh strainer or cheesecloth into a bowl. This will separate the milk solids from your cannabutter. Pour your cannabutter into a glass jar, ramekin or container of your choice and let it cool for 1 hour in the fridge. During this time the cannabutter will solidify and will be ready for use.

continues...

Butters, Oils & Extracts

Remove the cannabutter from the fridge and set out at room temperature until softened. Pour into a bowl and stir in the macerated strawberries and raw honey until fully combined. Place your Compound Strawberry Honey Cannabutter back into your container of choice and then back into the fridge for up to 3 months or in the freezer for up to 9 months.

Product Yield

This recipe for Compound Strawberry Honey Cannabutter produces 2 cups with 32 servings at 1 tablespoon each. Dose strength per tablespoon will be determined by what you choose from the dosing chart.

Basic Olive Oil

Directions

Determine your strain and proper dose of cannabis by referring to the dosing chart then set your bud aside in a bowl. On the stove, place the olive oil and ground cannabis into a pan then turn the stovetop on to the lowest setting. Make sure to completely stir in the ground cannabis so that it is totally covered by the oil. Cook this mixture on the lowest setting for 1 hour then remove from the heat and strain with a fine mesh strainer or cheesecloth into a measuring cup.

After the olive oil cools completely, pour into a sterilized glass bottle then secure the cap tightly. Store your cannabis-infused Basic Olive Oil in the refrigerator. This olive oil will have a shelf life of 1 month when refrigerated.

As a precaution, under no circumstances should the cannabis have any traces of moisture content left in it. Any amount of water, no matter how minute, will create the perfect environment in the oil to breed bacteria and can create toxins which may result in illnesses such as botulism. Make sure the cannabis is 100% cured before infusing. If at any point the bottle begins to cloud, throw it away immediately as this means sources of contamination have taken root in your oil.

Product Yield

This recipe for Basic Olive Oil produces 8 servings at 1 fluid ounce each. Your dose per serving will depend on the medication strength you pick from the dosing chart.

Mise en place

8 servings of dosed and ground strain of your choice*

8 fluid ounces olive oil

* Add the suggested amount of ground cannabis or alternative strain of ground cannabis of your choice by referring to the dosing chart on page 15 then the strain and alternative strains chart on page 7.

Dietary Lifestyle

O, OLV, OV, LV, P, V, GF

Rosemary Marjoram Infused Oil

Mise en place

8 servings of dosed and ground
strain of your choice*
8 fluid ounces olive oil
2 dried marjoram sprigs
1 dried rosemary sprig

Directions

Heat a pan on the stove on the lowest setting and add the olive oil then ground cannabis of your choice. Make sure to completely stir in the cannabis so that it is totally covered by the oil. Cook this mixture on the lowest setting for 1 hour then remove from heat and strain into a measuring cup.

While the olive oil is still warm, pour it from the measuring cup into a sterilized glass bottle. Add the sprigs of dried marjoram and rosemary then tightly seal. Let the olive oil and dried herbs infuse in the refrigerator for 2 weeks. At this point you can remove the sprigs of herbs to keep the current flavor or keep them in there for added decoration and deeper flavor. This Rosemary Marjoram Infused Oil will have a shelf life of 1 month when refrigerated.

As a precaution, under no circumstances should the herbs have any traces of moisture content left in them. Any amount of water, no matter how minute, will create the perfect environment in the oil to breed bacteria and can create toxins which may result in illnesses such as botulism. Make sure the herbs are 100% dried out before infusing. This same precaution is applied to the cannabis so make sure your bud is fully cured. If at any point the bottle begins to cloud, throw away immediately as this means water or other sources of contamination have taken root in your oil.

Product Yield

This recipe for Rosemary Marjoram Infused Oil produces 8 servings at 1 fluid ounce each. Your dose per serving will depend on the medication strength you pick from the dosing chart.

* Add the suggested amount of ground cannabis or alternative strain of ground cannabis of your choice by referring to the dosing chart on page 15 then the strain and alternative strains chart on page 7.

Dietary Lifestyle

O, OLV, OV, LV, P, V, GF

Raw Coconut Oil

Mise en place

32 servings of dosed and ground
strain of your choice*

2 cups raw coconut oil

Directions

Determine your strain and proper dose of cannabis by referring to the dosing chart then set your bud aside in a bowl. On the stove, place the raw coconut oil into a pan and turn the stovetop on to the lowest setting. Allow the coconut oil to melt then add in your ground cannabis strain and dosage of choice. Let this mixture infuse on the stove for 1 hour and stir the mixture every so often during this time.

After the hour is over, separate the ground cannabis from the mixture by running it through a fine mesh strainer or cheesecloth into a bowl. Pour your medicated Raw Coconut Oil into a glass jar and let it cool for 1 hour at room temperature. During this time the Raw Coconut Oil will solidify and will be ready for use. Place your jar in a cool dark place for up to 12 months.

As a precaution, under no circumstances should the buds have any trace of moisture content left in them. Any amount of moisture no matter how minute will create the perfect environment in the raw coconut oil to breed bacteria and can create toxins which may result in illnesses such as botulism. Make sure the buds are 100% cured before infusing. If at any time your medicated Raw Coconut Oil begins to smell bad, or you see spores developing, throw it away immediately. This means sources of contamination have taken root in your Raw Coconut Oil.

* Add the suggested amount of ground cannabis or alternative strain of ground cannabis of your choice by referring to the dosing chart on page 15 then the strain and alternative strains chart on page 7.

Dietary Lifestyle

O, OLV, OV, LV, P, V, GF

Product Yield

This recipe for Raw Coconut Oil produces 2 cups with 32 servings at 1 tablespoon each. Dose strength per tablespoon will be determined by what you choose from the dosing chart.

Butters, Oils & Extracts

Raw Coconut Honey

Mise en place

32 servings of dosed and ground
    strain of your choice*

1 cup raw coconut oil

1 cup raw honey

Directions

Determine your strain and proper dose of cannabis by referring to the dosing chart then set aside in a bowl. On the stove, place the raw coconut oil into a pan and turn the stovetop on to the lowest setting. Allow the coconut oil to melt then add in your ground cannabis strain and dosage of choice. Let this mixture infuse on the stove for 1 hour and stir every so often during this time frame. Keep in mind that the strain type you select will depend on which recipe you are using in this book.

* Add the suggested amount of ground cannabis or alternative strain of ground cannabis of your choice by referring to the dosing chart on page 15 then the strain and alternative strains chart on page 7.

Dietary Lifestyle

O, OLV, OV, LV, P, GF

After the hour is over, separate the ground cannabis from the mixture by running it through a fine mesh strainer or cheesecloth into a bowl. Place the bowl somewhere it can stand at room temperature and leave it covered until the oil solidifies fully. This may take anywhere from 30 minutes to 1 hour depending what temperature the room is.

In a mixing bowl, combine the infused raw coconut oil with the raw honey with a spoon until fully incorporated. Place into a container and store in a cool dark place for up to 12 months. It will be normal for the Raw Coconut Honey to crystalize or

even separate on the shelf if not used for many months. Simply warm in a hot pan over water or in the microwave then stir until uniform.

As a precaution, under no circumstances should the buds have any trace of moisture content left in them. Any amount of moisture no matter how minute will create the perfect environment in the raw coconut oil to breed bacteria and can create toxins which may result in illnesses such as botulism. Make sure the buds are 100% dried out/cured before infusing. If at any time your Raw Coconut Honey oil begins to smell bad or you see spores developing throw it away immediately. This means sources of contamination have taken root in your Raw Coconut Honey.

Product Yield

This recipe for Raw Coconut Honey produces 2 cups with 32 servings at 1 level tablespoon each. Dose strength per tablespoon will be determined by what you choose from the dosing chart.

Madagascar Vanilla Bean Bourbon Extract

Mise en place

48 servings of dosed and ground
strain of your choice*

¾ cup bourbon**

¼ cup water**

2 whole Madagascar vanilla beans**

8 fluid ounce glass jar**

Directions

Cut the vanilla beans lengthwise with a sharp knife and stop about ½ inch from the end. Now pour both the bourbon and water into the 8 fluid ounce glass jar. Grind the cannabis into a fine powder and add into the jar. Lastly, add in the two Madagascar vanilla beans before closing the jar.

Take the jar and place it into a cool dark cupboard for a period of 8 weeks to infuse. During this time you must shake the jar vigorously once a week for approximately 30 seconds. After the 8 week period, strain the mixture through a fine mesh strainer into a cup. Clean out the 8 fluid ounce glass jar with water only and then pour the extract back into the jar.

You can use this extract for baking, cooking and making drinks. This extract will last indefinitely as long as you store it in a cool dark place and make sure the lid is properly sealed. If you wish to sweeten this extract you may add in 2-3 tablespoons of corn syrup and shake the jar until fully incorporated.

Product Yield

This recipe for Madagascar Vanilla Bean Bourbon Extract produces 1 cup with 48 servings at 1 teaspoon each.** Dose strength per teaspoon will be determined by what you choose from the dosing chart.

* Add the suggested amount of ground cannabis or alternative strain of ground cannabis of your choice by referring to the dosing chart on page 15 then the strain and alternative strains chart on page 7.

**These values may need to be doubled or tripled if you are using higher doses of cannabis based on the dosing chart to extract from. Regardless, if you double or triple, this recipe will still produce a serving of 1 teaspoon each.

Dietary Lifestyle

O, OLV, OV, LV, P, V, GF

Lightly Medicated Basic Honey Peanut Butter

Mise en place

1½ cups raw, unsalted peanuts
1 fluid ounce Basic Olive Oil*
1-3 tablespoons of honey
Pinch of sea salt

Directions

On a large cookie sheet, roast the raw, unsalted peanuts at 350°F for 25 minutes. Mix the peanuts with a spoon at the 15-minute mark to ensure proper heat distribution. Pull from the oven after the full 25 minutes is over and add to your food processor.

Add the Basic Olive Oil, honey and sea salt into the food processor and mix at intervals until the desired consistency is reached.

Because this product has no preservatives like most mass-produced nut butters, you need to store it in the fridge. Place the Lightly Medicated Basic Honey Peanut Butter in an airtight container in the fridge. This product will have a shelf life of 2 months when stored this way. Set the product out at room temperature for 15 minutes before serving to soften up.

Product Yield

This recipe for Lightly Medicated Basic Honey Peanut Butter produces 1½ cups with 12 servings per container at 2 level tablespoons per serving. Your dose per serving will depend on the medication strength you pick from the dosing chart.

Take into account that this designed for light medication and each serving will have very minimal in cannabis. If you wish to have a specific, consistent dose per serving, you will need to add 1 fluid ounce of non-medicated oil and your preferred dose of decarboxylated kief of your chosen strain by referring to the dosing chart.

* Follow the recipe for Basic Olive Oil on page 35 and add the desired dose of any cannabis strain by referring to the dosing chart on page 15.

Dietary Lifestyle

O, OLV, OV, LV, P, GF

Lightly Medicated Basic Hazelnut Butter

Mise en place

1½ cups chopped hazelnuts
1 cup semi-sweet chocolate chips
1 fluid ounce Basic Olive Oil*
Pinch of sea salt

Directions

On a large cookie sheet, roast the chopped hazelnuts at 350°F for 25 minutes. Mix the hazelnuts with a spoon at the 15-minute mark to ensure proper heat distribution. Pull from the oven after the full 25 minutes is over and add to your food processor.

Add in the semi-sweet chocolate chips, Basic Olive Oil and sea salt. How viscous you want your hazelnut butter to be will determine how much oil to put in. Start by adding one tablespoon and run the food processor for 1 minute. If you wish for the mixture to have a little more flow, add in 1 to 2 more tablespoons of oil and run the food processor for another minute. Continue to run the food processor until all of the mixture is fully incorporated. In this specific recipe I added 3 tablespoons as I feel it creates the perfect consistency.

Because this product has no preservatives like most mass-produced nut butters, you need to store it in the fridge. Place the Lightly Medicated Basic Hazelnut Butter in an airtight container in the fridge. This product will have a shelf life of 2 months when stored this way. Set the product out at room temperature for 15 minutes before serving to soften up.

Product Yield

This recipe for Lightly Medicated Basic Hazelnut Butter produces 2½ cups with 20 servings per container at 2 level tablespoons per serving. Your dose per serving will depend on the medication strength you pick from the dosing chart.

Take into account that this recipe is designed for light medication. If you wish to have a specific, consistent dose per serving, you will need to add 1 fluid ounce of non-medicated oil and your preferred dose of decarboxylated kief of your chosen strain by referring to the dosing chart.

* Follow the recipe for Basic Olive Oil on page 35 and add the desired dose of any cannabis strain by referring to the dosing chart on page 15.

Dietary Lifestyle

O, OLV, OV, LV, P, GF

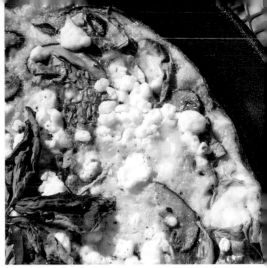

Breakfast & Brunch

Warm Honey HeadBand Klef Walnuts in
Greek Yogurt

Bajan Silver Haze Sweet Bread

Jewish American Caramella Coffee Cake

English Lavender Buttermilk Currant Scones

Americana Elvis Pancakes

Strawberry Haze French Toast

Jewish American NYC Diesel Lox Bagel

Italian Diabolic Funxta Eggs in Purgatory

Venezuelan Haze Scrambled Eggs

Italian Exodus Cheese Frittata

Warm Honey Headband Kief Walnuts in Greek Yogurt

In Greece, yogurt, honey and nuts play huge roles throughout many various dishes. Greek yogurt is traditionally served with honey poured over the top or even plain. But why not pair rich Greek yogurt with the warm sweet tones of honey, and the earthy deep tones of headband kief and walnuts? This is sure to please as a morning treat to get you up and going for the day.

Directions

In a saucepan over a medium low heat, combine the honey, walnuts, cinnamon and lemon juice and cook for 10 minutes. Make sure to stir every few minutes to prevent clumping in the pan. At the end of your 10 minutes, pull from the stove and immediately add the kief. Pour this mixture equally over 4 individual cups of Greek yogurt.

Product Yield

This recipe for Warm Honey HeadBand Kief Walnuts in Greek Yogurt produces 4 servings. Dose strength per serving will be determined by what you choose from the dosing chart.

Mise en place

4 cups plain Greek yogurt

4 servings of dosed decarboxylated HeadBand kief*

1 cup raw whole shelled walnuts

½ cup clover honey

1 teaspoon cinnamon

1 teaspoon lemon juice

* Add the desired dose of decarboxylated HeadBand kief or alternative decarboxylated strain kief into this dish per serving by referring to the dosing chart on page 15 and decarboxylation process on page 16.

Dietary Lifestyle

O, OLV, LV, P, GF

Bajan Silver Haze Sweet Bread

This is one of the most popular traditional sweet breads on the Caribbean island of Barbados. It is a favorite among all Barbadians and is served for breakfast with tea. The fruity pine notes of Silver Haze bring out the sweetness from this bread while the cool menthol undertones balance with the tartness of the cherries.

Directions

In a bowl add the flour, coconut, egg, cherries, sugar, Basic Clarified Silver Haze Cannabutter, almond extract, vanilla extract, baking powder, sea salt and only ½ of the cup of milk. Stir this mixture until incorporated then add the other half of the milk and stir until fully combined. Grease a loaf pan with 2 teaspoon of raw coconut oil, then pour the sweet bread batter into it.

Bake your Bajan Silver Haze Sweet Bread at 350°F for 40 minutes. Pull from the oven after the 40 minutes is up and spread your Silver Haze Raw Coconut Honey over the sweet bread. Cut into 6 pieces which can be served warm out of the oven or at room temperature.

Product Yield

This recipe for Bajan Silver Haze Sweet Bread produces 6 servings. Dose strength per slice will be determined by what you choose from the dosing chart.

Mise en place

2 cups all-purpose flour

1¼ cup grated coconut fresh or dry

1 cup condensed unsweetened milk

1 egg

⅔ cup dried sweetened cherries

½ cup turbinado sugar

¼ cup Basic Clarified Silver Haze Cannabutter*

2 tablespoons Silver Haze Raw Coconut Honey*

2 teaspoons almond extract

2 teaspoons vanilla extract

1 teaspoon non-medicated raw coconut oil

½ teaspoon baking powder

½ teaspoon sea salt

* Follow the recipe for Basic Clarified Cannabutter on page 27 and Raw Coconut Honey on page 41 and add the desired dose of Silver Haze or alternative strain by referring to the dosing chart on page 15.

Dietary Lifestyle

O, OLV, P

Jewish American Caramella Coffee Cake

Mise en place

Coffee cakes are one of the many pleasures when it comes to choosing something sweet to eat for breakfast. This recipe is traditional in many Jewish American homes and is served for breakfast or during the holidays. The sweet caramel candy tone of the Caramella strain heightens the sweet notes of the coffee cake. Serve with hot coffee or tea for a delicious, light breakfast.

Directions

Add the flour, eggs, sugar, baking soda, sea salt, vanilla extract, almond extract, sour cream, room temperature non-medicated butter and 10 servings of dosed ground Caramella. Set the bowl aside and move to the next step for the crumb mixture.

10 servings of dosed ground Caramella*

3 eggs

2 cups all-purpose flour

1 cup sour cream

1 stick room temperature non-medicated butter

1 cup white sugar

1 teaspoon vanilla extract

1 teaspoon almond extract

1 teaspoon baking soda

⅛ teaspoon sea salt

Crumb Mixture

¾ cup brown sugar

½ cup chopped raw walnuts

2 tablespoons softened non-medicated butter

2 teaspoons vanilla extract

In a small bowl, add the brown sugar, room temperature non-medicated butter, walnuts and vanilla extract. Stir the mixture until it comes together in a moist crumble mixture.

continues...

* Add the desired dose of Caramella or alternative strain by referring to the dosing chart on page 15.

Dietary Lifestyle

O, OLV, P

Pour half the batter into a greased 9-inch cake pan then sprinkle half of the crumble mixture over the batter. Then pour the other half of the batter into the pan followed by the other half of the crumble mixture.

Bake in a preheated oven at 350°F for 45 to 50 minutes or until a toothpick inserted comes out clean. Cool the cake then lightly dust with confectioners' sugar to serve.

Product Yield

This recipe for Jewish American Caramella Coffee Cake produces 10 servings. Your dose per serving will depend on the medication strength you pick from the dosing chart.

English Lavender Buttermilk Currant Scones

Scones are traditional British fare, especially when served with tea, and they are Scottish in origin. Lavender is the perfect strain to compliment this dish as it adds a deep hash flavor with undertones of lavender. These flavors mingle by elevating the mildly sweet and tangy scone to bring about a slightly complex flavor.

Directions

In a large mixing bowl add the flours, egg, currants, orange zest, lemon zest, sugar, baking powder, baking soda, sea salt, Basic Clarified Lavender Cannabutter, vanilla extract, and ¾ cup buttermilk. Stir this mixture until it is well combined and a sticky dough begins to form.

Mise en place

1 cup wheat flour

1 cup all-purpose flour

1 egg

¾ cup buttermilk plus ¼ cup reserve

½ cup room temperature Basic Clarified Lavender Cannabutter*

½ dried currants

¼ cup turbinado sugar

Zest from 1 orange and 1 lemon

2 teaspoons non-medicated vanilla extract

1½ teaspoon baking powder

½ teaspoon sea salt

¼ teaspoon baking soda

*Follow the recipe for Basic Clarified Cannabutter on page 27 and add the desired dose of Lavender or alternative strain by referring to the dosing chart on page 15.

Dietary Lifestyle

O, OLV, P

Flour a cutting board then place the dough on top. Lightly sprinkle the top of the dough with some more flour and gently pat into an even circle. Slice the dough in to 8 wedges as shown and transfer to a baking sheet. Evenly space the wedges and

then rub each scone with ¼ cup reserved buttermilk. Place into a preheated oven of 375°F then bake for 15 to 20 minutes or until lightly golden and firm to the touch.

In a small bowl mix the confectioners' sugar, vanilla extract, almond extract and water until it forms a glaze. If you find it is too thick for your liking, you can thin it out by adding 1 teaspoon of water at a time until you reach your desired consistency. If you find it is too thin, then slowly add 1 tablespoon of confectioners' sugar until it reaches your desired consistency.

Fully cool the scones then drizzle the glaze over them. Let the glaze fully dry then serve with warm tea of your choice.

Product Yield

This recipe for English Lavender Buttermilk Currant Scones produces 8 servings. Dose strength per serving will be determined by what you choose from the dosing chart.

Mise en place
Glaze
1 cup confectioners' sugar
1 teaspoon vanilla extract
1 teaspoon almond extract
1 fluid ounce water

Americana Elvis Pancakes

Pancakes and Elvis are both parts of traditional Americana. Naturally, I wanted to combine my love of pancakes with Elvis' love of peanut butter, banana and bacon sandwiches, and what makes this recipe even better is the addition of the Elvis strain. Thus, Americana Elvis Pancakes were born.

Directions

Fry the fresh bacon in a skillet until crispy then drain and blot dry with a paper towel. You can also use precooked or leftover bacon to substitute for fresh bacon. Use 4 to 8 slices depending on your preference. In a large bowl add all of your dry ingredients plus the chocolate chips and chopped bacon and give it a few gentle stirs with a whisk

In the same bowl add the egg, melted Basic Clarified Elvis Cannabutter, milk, vanilla and almond extract. Stir this mixture with a whisk until smooth and fully combined. Cut up the bananas into this mixture and gently fold until evenly distributed.

If you used a skillet to make fresh bacon use the same pan but pour out the bacon grease. Do not clean out the skillet as you want the bacon flavor to infuse into the pancakes. Turn your stovetop to the medium low setting and pour about ¼ cup of batter into the skillet. Cook for about 2 to 3 minutes or until the top of the pancake is filled with tiny bubbles. Then flip the pancake and cook for another 2 to 3 minutes. You can do multiple pancakes at the same time depending on how much room you have in the skillet. As you make them, pile the pancakes onto a plate and cover with another plate to keep them warm. Serve with maple syrup, maple agave nectar or melted honey.

Product Yield

This recipe creates 8 Americana Elvis Pancakes with 4 servings of 2 pancakes per serving. Your dose per serving will depend on the medication strength you pick from the dosing chart.

Mise en place

4 to 8 slices of bacon

2 small bananas

1 ¼ cup all-purpose flour

1 cup milk

¼ cup chocolate chips

1 egg

4 tablespoons of melted Basic Clarified Elvis Cannabutter*

1 tablespoon sugar

1 teaspoon vanilla extract

1 teaspoon almond extract

1 teaspoon baking powder

½ teaspoon baking soda

* Follow the recipe for Basic Clarified Cannabutter on page 27 and add the desired dose of Strawberry Haze or alternative strain by referring to the dosing chart on page 15.

Dietary Lifestyle

O

Strawberry Haze French Toast

French Toast as a dish has its roots in many places, from Brazil to Portugal and many other European countries. Taking French toast and stepping it up to the next level results in stuffed French toast which many people all over the world enjoy. The sweet strawberry and rose petal notes of Strawberry Haze add an extra unique strawberry flavor that brings immense pleasure to the senses in the overall dish

Directions

In a small ramekin combine the cream cheese and Compound Strawberry Haze Honey Cannabutter then set aside. In a medium sized bowl add the eggs, milk, vanilla extract, almond extract and cinnamon. Whisk this mixture until all ingredients have been incorporated.

Mise en place

8 slices challah bread

5 eggs

1 banana

4 fluid ounces cream cheese

¼ cup milk

4 tablespoons Compound
   Strawberry Haze Honey
   Cannabutter*

1 teaspoon vanilla extract

1 teaspoon almond extract

1 teaspoon ground cinnamon

Maple syrup or agave nectar to
   garnish

* Follow the recipe for the Compound Strawberry Honey Cannabutter on page 31 and add the desired dose of Strawberry Haze or alternative strain by referring to the dosing chart on page 15.

Dietary Lifestyle
O, OLV, P

Next take two slices of challah bread and spread 2.5 fluid ounces of the medicated cream cheese strawberry compound butter spread onto both sides evenly and

equally. Thinly slice the banana and lay down the amount you want keeping in mind you need to save enough slices for 3 other servings. Press the challah bread slices together and dip both sides into the egg wash mixture.

Quickly lay the stuffed strawberry haze French toast onto a non-stick medium hot pan and allow one side to cook for 3 to 4 minutes or until golden brown. Repeat on the other side of the French toast and then plate. Drizzle with maple syrup or agave nectar.

Product Yield

This recipe for Strawberry Haze French Toast produces 4 servings. Your dose per serving will depend on the medication strength you pick from the dosing chart.

Jewish American NYC Diesel Lox Bagel

Lox bagels are a traditional part of Ashkenazi Jewish cuisine and have been passed down to many Jewish American families from their central and eastern European relatives. These bagels are also hugely popular on the east coast and can be found in many delis across New York State. The tart, diesel and citrus flavors of NYC Diesel meld perfectly with the flavors of the lox bagel.

Directions

Cut the bagels in halves then toast them until they reach the level of doneness you prefer. Take 1 bagel slice then spread 1 tablespoon of Clarified Herbed NYC Diesel Cannabutter onto the slice. Repeat this process for the rest of the bagel halves so that each bagel half has 1 tablespoon of Clarified Herbed NYC Diesel Cannabutter spread onto it. Then spread 1 ounce of cream cheese onto each of the 6 bagel halves. Lay 1 slice of lox, 2 thinly sliced red onion rounds and 2 thinly sliced lemon rounds onto each bagel half. Season each bagel half with cracked pepper and garnish with capers.

Product Yield

This recipe for Jewish American NYC Diesel Lox Bagel produces 6 servings. Dose strength per serving will be determined by what you choose from the dosing chart.

Mise en place

12 thinly sliced red onion rounds

12 thinly sliced lemons rounds

6 slices lox (cured salmon)

6 ounces cream cheese

6 tablespoons of Clarified Herbed NYC Diesel Cannabutter*

3 large everything bagels

Cracked pepper and capers to garnish

* Follow the recipe for Clarified Herbed Cannabutter on page 29 and add the desired dose of NYC Diesel or alternative strain by referring to the dosing chart on page 15.

Dietary Lifestyle

O, P

Italian Diabolic Funxta Eggs in Purgatory

This is a classic dish that originated in Naples, Italy, and it is the perfect comfort food for breakfast. Because Diabolic Funxta is a diesel-tasting strain with heavy floral and citrus notes, it pairs perfectly with the red sauce in this dish. When the creamy rich egg hits your palate with the red sauce it will send your taste buds on a thrill ride.

Directions

In a large frying pan place the ½ cup tomato paste with 1 cup water. Over a medium low heat stir this mixture until well combined. Add in the Parmesan cheese, dried onions, Italian seasoning, garlic and sugar. Now add in your fresh basil and Basic Clarified Diabolic Funxta Cannabutter. Stir these ingredients into the sauce and let it simmer on medium for 15 minutes.

Mise en place

4 eggs

1 cup water

½ cup tomato paste

¼ cup fresh basil

½ cup shredded mozzarella cheese

¼ cup Basic Diabolic Funxta Olive Oil*

3 minced garlic cloves

2 tablespoons Parmesan cheese

2 tablespoons dried onions

2 tablespoons Italian seasoning

2 tablespoons sugar

2 tablespoons Basic Clarified
   Diabolic Funxta Cannabutter*

Sea Salt and Black Pepper to taste if
   desired

* Follow the recipe for Basic Clarified Cannabutter on page 27 and Basic Olive Oil on page 35 and add the desired dose of Diabolic Funxta or alternative strain by referring to the dosing chart on page 15.

Dietary Lifestyle

O, OLV, P

After 15 minutes of simmering, add in your Basic Diabolic Funxta Olive Oil by drizzling it into the sauce, but do not stir it in. Crack 4 eggs into the sauce with enough space between them all to prevent the eggs from baking into each other. Cook on

medium low until the eggs reach your preference or until the eggs are fully cooked which takes 8 to 10 minutes.

Take the pan off the stove and sprinkle the shredded mozzarella cheese on top of the sauce. Season this dish with sea salt and crushed red pepper if desired before serving. You can serve this dish family style in the pan accompanied with fresh baked bread for a rustic style or simply serve independently.

Product Yield

This recipe for Italian Diabolic Funxta Eggs in Purgatory produces 4 servings. Dose strength per serving will be determined by what you choose from the dosing chart.

Venezuelan Haze Scrambled Eggs

Venezuelan scrambled eggs have their history as a traditional and very popular breakfast that are served with arepas. Traditionally this dish is called "Perico" which comes from the Spanish word for parrot. The strong pine, Skunk and earth tones of Haze balance in harmony with the flavors of this dish.

Directions

Set a saucepan over a low heat and place the olive oil and ground Haze into it. Make sure the cannabis is fully covered and immersed in the oil. The amount of cannabis you use in this recipe will depend on your dose per serving. If you are making this recipe with a higher dose per serving you may find that the oil will not cover all of the cannabis. If this is the case, add 1 shot of vodka to the mixture. Do not worry about alcohol being in this recipe as it will cook out of the food by the time the cooking time is over.

Continue to cook this mixture on the lowest setting for 45 minutes. After the 45 minutes is up roughly chop the tomatoes, garlic, sweet bell pepper, and onion. Add to the pan and cook for 10 minutes on medium low. Break the eggs into a bowl and whisk them for about 2 minutes until well incorporated with air. Pour the whisked eggs on top of the vegetable mixture and wait for the eggs to set before scrambling, which should last around a minute. Scramble the eggs until they are firm, moist and fluffy. Season with sea salt and pepper, garnish with fresh basil and serve with warmed arepas.

Product Yield

This recipe for Venezuelan Haze Scrambled Eggs produces 4 servings. Your dose per serving will depend on the medication strength you pick from the dosing chart.

Mise en place

6 whole eggs
4 servings of dosed ground Haze*
2 globe tomatoes
2 cloves garlic
1 green sweet bell pepper
1 sweet onion
1 fluid ounce non-medicated olive oil
Sea salt and pepper to taste

* Add the desired dose of Haze or alternative strain by referring to the dosing chart on page 15.

Dietary Lifestyle

O, OLV, OV, P, GF

Italian Exodus Cheese Frittata

The term "Frittata" originally was a general term in Italy for cooking or frying eggs in a skillet. Frittatas are known as open face Italian omelets that are usually served for breakfast. Exodus Cheese lends an earthy cheese flavor that tastes as if another cheese has been placed into the Frittata besides the goat cheese. Serve with your favorite cup of coffee or tea and a glass of orange juice for a great breakfast.

Directions

In a large glass bowl, whip the eggs with a whisk until well incorporated with air. Add the minced onion, garlic, sliced tomato, portabella mushrooms, ground cannabis, olive oil and spinach into the bowl. Fold this mixture with a whisk until everything is well combined.

Pour into seasoned cast iron skillet or one that has been oiled with non-medicated olive oil. Sprinkle the goat cheese across the egg mixture and garnish with 6 large

Mise en place

12 eggs

8 servings of dosed decarboxylated ground Exodus Cheese*

6 large fresh basil leaves

4 baby sliced portabella mushrooms

1 large sweet onion minced

1 large tomato

1 cup fresh spinach

1 clove minced garlic (optional)

⅓ cup goat cheese

¼ cup non-medicated olive oil

* Add the desired dose of decarboxylated Exodus or alternative decarboxylated strain into this dish per serving by referring to the dosing chart on page 15 and decarboxylation process on page 16.

Dietary Lifestyle

O, OLV, P

basil leaves. Bake uncovered in the center of the oven at 350°F for 35 minutes. Pull from the oven then slice into 8 sections and serve.

Product Yield

This recipe for Italian Exodus Cheese Frittata produces 8 servings. Your dose per serving will depend on the medication strength you pick from the dosing chart.

Lunch

American Blue Pearl Ahi Tuna Sandwich

Thai Mako Haze Kief Beef Salad

Indian Mandala #1 Curried Chickpeas

Chinese Chicken Mekong High Lettuce Cups

Lebanese Sour Diesel Tabouli

American B-52 Reuben Sandwich

The Third Dimension Cuban Sandwich

American Yumboldt Chicken Club Sandwich

Polish Open Face Cheesus Sandwich

English Cucumber Speed Queen Sandwich

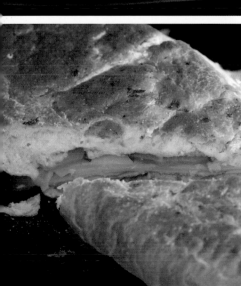

American Blue Pearl Ahi Tuna Sandwich

Ahi tuna is actually a yellowfin tuna, which is one of the largest tuna species and can weigh around 300 pounds. Ahi is a term used by Hawaiians to refer to yellowfin or bigeye tuna. This sandwich captures the Hawaiian flair and can be found across the United States in many restaurants. The refreshing lemon and citrus tones of Blue Pearl deepen the flavors of the sauce in this recipe, creating the perfect tropical flavor for the Ahi tuna.

Directions

In a frying pan, place ¼ cup orange juice, ¼ cup lemon juice and 4 tablespoons Basic Raw Blue Pearl Coconut Honey. Stir on low until the honey has dissolved completely in the juice. Now add your Ahi tuna steaks, sliced garlic, cayenne pepper and season with sea salt and pepper. With the heat on medium high, cook each steak for 6 minutes on each side for rare steaks, or longer for your desired doneness.

Mise en place

4 (4 ounce) Ahi tuna

4 bread buns

2 avocados

1 red onion

1 garlic clove

1 cup spring salad mix

¼ cup orange juice

¼ cup lemon juice plus 4 tablespoons reserve

4 tablespoons Basic Raw Blue Pearl Coconut Honey*

⅛ teaspoon cayenne pepper

Sea salt and ground pepper to season

While the Ahi tuna is cooking, place the avocados in a bowl with 4 tablespoons lemon juice reserve. Season the avocados with sea salt and pepper, then mash. Slice

*Follow the recipe for Basic Raw Coconut Honey on page 41 and add the desired dose of Blue Pearl or alternative strain by referring to the dosing chart on page 15.

Dietary Lifestyle

O, P

the bread (you may toast the bread if desired) and onions then spread the avocado mixture on each side of the 8 bread slices. Divide the spring salad mix into 4 portions and place on the bottom half of each sandwich. Place the Ahi Tuna slices on top of the spring salad mix and then quickly return to the pan with just the juice and honey mixture to the stove. Turn up the heat to high and cook for several minutes so that the remaining sauce reduces. Evenly divide this sauce into 4 servings then spoon over each Ahi tuna steak and then top with the desired amount of sliced red onions. Add the top of your bun and press lightly to glue your sandwich together then serve.

Product Yield

This recipe for American Blue Pearl Ahi Tuna Sandwich produces 4 servings. Dose strength per serving will be determined by what you choose from the dosing chart.

Thai Mako Haze Kief Beef Salad

Thai beef salad or "yum nua" is a traditional sour salad made in Thailand. This is a very refreshing dish full of exotic flavors that many do not get to experience. The exotic flavors combine beautifully with the earthy sandalwood and spice of Mako Haze kief to produce a vivid dish.

Directions

In a frying pan, place your steak cut of choice then season with sea salt and pepper. Cook the meat for 3 minutes on each side for rare steaks, or until desired doneness. Set the meat aside to rest while you prepare the other components of the salad.

Combine all the salad dressing ingredients together in a ramekin, then stir in

Mise en place

1 pound steak cut of your choice

8 ounces romaine lettuce hearts

4 servings of dosed decarboxylated
    Mako Haze Kief*

2 plum tomatoes

1 red onion

1 cucumber

¼ fresh mint leaves

¼ cup Thai basil

Sea salt and pepper to season

* Add the desired dose of decarboxylated Mako Haze Kief or alternative decarboxylated kief into this dish per serving by referring to the dosing chart on page 15 and decarboxylation process on page 16.

Dietary Lifestyle

O, GF (make sure sweet chili sauce and fish sauce are labeled as GF)

Lunch

4 servings of dosed decarboxylated Mako Haze Kief. Slice or tear the romaine hearts, mint leaves and Thai basil leaves then place in a large salad bowl. Slice the cucumbers and tomatoes then add to the bowl. Pour the salad dressing over the vegetables and gently toss with two spoons until evenly coated.

Slice your rested meat and red onion. Plate the salad greens then add the desired amount of red onion. Divide the meat up into 4 servings then place on top of each plated salad portion.

Product Yield

This recipe for Thai Mako Haze Kief Beef Salad produces 4 servings. Dose strength per serving will be determined by what you choose from the dosing chart.

Mise en place

Salad Dressing

Combine in a Ramekin:

2 fluid ounces non-medicated olive oil

2 minced garlic cloves

4 tablespoons sweet chili sauce

2 tablespoons lime juice

2 tablespoons brown sugar

1 teaspoon fish sauce

Indian Mandala #1 Curried Chickpeas

Various forms of curried chickpeas can be found all over India, each one using different combinations of spices and herbs according to the area. Mandala #1 encompasses a strong citrus taste with smoky earth tones that brings a great undertone of flavors behind the spices and herbs. Serve alone with goat cheese or paneer for a lunch dish that is loaded with antioxidants. You can also scoop up the chickpeas with oven naan for a delicious hand wrap.

Directions

Drain and then rinse the canned chickpeas and place them in a paella pan or other large pan. Pour the melted Mandala #1 Raw Coconut Oil or non-medicated raw

Mise en place

1 (15 ounce) can of chickpeas

2 cloves garlic minced

1 tomato

1 sweet onion

1 cup spinach

¼ cup water reserve

¼ cup crumbled goat cheese or paneer

4 tablespoons melted Mandala #1 Raw Coconut Oil or non-medicated raw coconut oil*

4 servings dosed ground decarboxylated Mandala #1**

2 teaspoons curry powder

1 teaspoon each of cumin, coriander, paprika, ginger, and turmeric

⅛ teaspoon cayenne pepper

* Follow the recipe for Raw Coconut Oil on page 39 and add the desired dose of Mandala #1 or alternative strain by referring to the dosing chart on page 15.
**Add the desired dose of decarboxylated Mandala #1 or alternative strain by referring to the dosing chart on page 15 if you choose not to use the Mandala #1 Raw Coconut Oil.

Dietary Lifestyle

O, OLV, LV, P

coconut oil* over them. Then add the minced garlic, spices and spinach. Coarsely chop the onion and tomato then add to the pan.

If you choose to add in the non-medicated raw coconut oil in the previous step because you want to use decarboxylated Mandala #1, then add in the 4 servings of decarboxylated Mandala #1**. Cook this mixture on medium high while constantly stirring for 10 to 12 minutes or until onions become translucent and vegetables reduce. If at any time your vegetable mixture becomes too dry during the cooking process, add ¼ cup water from your reserve to moisten. Sprinkle crumbled goat cheese or paneer over the top and serve.

Product Yield

This recipe for Indian Mandala #1 Curried Chickpeas produces 4 servings. Dose strength per serving will be determined by what you choose from the dosing chart.

Chinese Chicken Mekong High Lettuce Cups

Chinese chicken cups have distant origins in Fujianese cooking but traditionally used squab instead of chicken. You can tailor this dish by adding the spicy and heavy earth tones of Mekong High to create very robust chicken cups. If you prefer, you can use the lightly sweet and floral taste of the ABV to make the chicken cups a little more on the sweet side. The choice is left to you but either is sure to make your taste buds very happy.

Directions

In a paella pan or wok, place the coarsely chopped sweet onion, bell pepper, mushrooms, orange rind, Basic Clarified Mekong High Cannabutter or non-medicated butter*, ginger, red pepper flakes, sea salt, garlic and hoisin sauce. If you

Mise en place

1 pound minced chicken
2 green onions to garnish
2 cloves minced garlic
1 small head of Boston Bibb lettuce
1 large sweet onion
1 small sweet red bell pepper
1 cup shitake mushrooms
¼ cup hoisin sauce
4 tablespoons Basic Clarified Mekong High Cannabutter OR 4 tablespoons non-medicated butter* with 4 servings of dosed ABV cannabis**
Rind of 1 orange
1 teaspoon ground ginger
1 teaspoon red pepper flakes
Few dashes Sea Salt

* Follow the recipe for Basic Clarified Cannabutter on page 27 and add the desired dose of Mekong High or alternative strain by referring to the dosing chart on page 15.
**Add the desired dose of the ABV (already been vaped) cannabis by referring to the dosing chart on page 15 if you choose not to use the Basic Clarified Mekong High Cannabutter.

Dietary Lifestyle

O, GF (make sure hoisin sauce is labeled GF)

choose to add in the non-medicated butter in the previous step because you want to use ABV cannabis, then add in the 4 servings of dosed ABV cannabis**.

Sauté the vegetable mixture until translucent and tender then add in the minced chicken. Cook the meat until thoroughly done and pull from the heat. Gently peel leaves off the Boston Bibb lettuce head and spoon the chicken mixture into these lettuce cups. Chop up the green onions and garnish each lettuce cup with these to serve.

Product Yield

This recipe for Chinese Chicken Mekong High Lettuce Cups produces 4 servings Dose strength per serving will be determined by what you choose from the dosing chart.

Lebanese Sour Diesel Tabouli

Tabouli is Levantine in origin and has become one of the most popular salads in the Middle East. Sour Diesel is the perfect strain to enhance the earthy and fresh flavors of this dish. The sourness, lemon, and pine boost the herbs and vegetables in this dish creating an exciting array of taste profiles. Enjoy by itself, or with fresh pita, hummus or baba ghanoush.

Directions

Place the bulgur and hot water in a bowl, allowing this mixture to soak for 30 minutes. After the 30 minutes is up, drain the bulgur and place into a new bowl. Add the cucumber, tomato, garlic, green onions, Basic Sour Diesel Olive Oil, lemon

Mise en place

2 cups hot water

2 green onions diced

2 cloves garlic minced

1 large tomato diced

1 small cucumber diced

¾ cup bulgur

½ cup fresh lemon juice

½ cup Basic Sour Diesel Olive Oil*

¼ cup minced fresh mint

¼ cup minced fresh parsley

Sea salt and pepper to taste

* Follow the recipe for Basic Olive Oil on page 35 and add the desired dose of Sour Diesel or alternative strain by referring to the dosing chart on page 15.

Dietary Lifestyle

O, OLV, OV, LV, P, V

juice, mint and parsley. Stir the mixture with a spoon until fully incorporated then season with sea salt and pepper.

Cover the bowl and place in the fridge for 30 minutes for the flavors to develop and deepen. You can serve chilled or at room temperature.

Product Yield

This recipe for Lebanese Sour Diesel Tabouli produces 4 servings. Your dose per serving will depend on the medication strength you pick from the dosing chart.

American B-52 Reuben Sandwich

The original Reuben sandwich was supposedly created in Omaha, Nebraska by a Lithuanian-born grocer by the name of Reuben Kulakofsky. Though other stories of possible creators surround this sandwich, I know one thing for sure, and that is how delicious this sandwich is. The sweet pine taste of B-52 with Skunk and lemon notes compliments the corned beef, sauerkraut, Swiss cheese and Thousand Island dressing for a mouthwatering sandwich.

Mise en place

16 slices corned beef

16 slices Swiss cheese

8 slices rye bread

1 cup sauerkraut

½ cup thousand island dressing

4 tablespoons Clarified Herbed B-52
   Cannabutter*

1 tablespoon garlic powder

Directions

Lay the bread slices onto a pan or cutting board to use as a workspace. Spread 1 tablespoon of Thousand Island dressing onto each slice of bread then place one slice of Swiss cheese onto the dressed slices. Take 4 of these slices and place aside then lay 4 slices of corned beef onto each of the remaining slices. Divide the sauerkraut and place on top of each of the 4 slices of corned beef, then take the remaining bread slices and top off these ingredients.

Now take your 4 sandwiches and spread 1 tablespoon of Clarified Herbed B-52 Cannabutter onto both sides of each sandwich. Lightly sprinkle the garlic powder on all sides of each sandwich then place them in a hot pan or skillet on medium heat. Grill each side for 5 to 8 minutes or until each side is golden brown. Slice diagonally and serve with a pickle or chips.

* Follow the recipe for Clarified Herbed Cannabutter on page 29 and add the desired dose of B-52 or alternative strain by referring to the dosing chart on page 15.

Dietary Lifestyle

O

Product Yield

This recipe for American B-52 Reuben Sandwich produces 4 servings. Dose strength per serving will be determined by what you choose from the dosing chart.

Lunch

The Third Dimension Cuban Sandwich

Mise en place

Cuban sandwiches were created in cafes that catered to Cuban sugar mill and cigar factory works in immigrant communities in Florida as well as in Cuba itself. The tart lemon tones of the Third Dimension strain really tie the whole sandwich together creating an overall savory taste profile.

16 ounces of pulled pork

2 small loves of Cuban or French bread

8 slices of ham

8 slices of Swiss cheese

6 large spears of bread and butter pickles

⅓ cup mustard

4 tablespoons Basic Clarified The Third Dimension Cannabutter*

Directions

Cut the 2 small loves in half longthwise and lay onto a metal sheet pan. Spread the mustard onto all 4 slices until evenly coated then divide the pulled pork onto 2 of the slices. Then lay 4 slices of ham and Swiss cheese on top of the pulled

* Follow the recipe for Basic Clarified Cannabutter on page 27 and add the desired dose of The Third Dimension or alternative strain by referring to the dosing chart on page 15.

Dietary Lifestyle
O

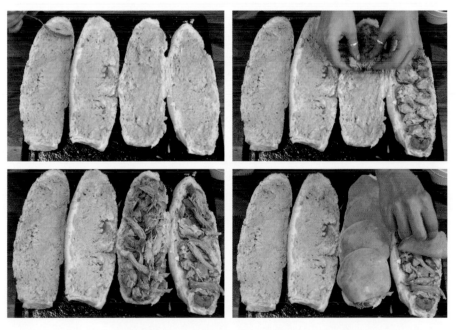

pork. Slice the pickles and divide between these 2 slices and then add the tops to make a sandwich.

Spread 2 tablespoons of Basic Clarified The Third Dimension Cannabutter onto each sandwich making sure to evenly coat the top and bottom outside slices. You can now leave these sandwiches on the sheet pan and place a heavy skillet over them to broil them in the oven. If you choose to use this method, broil the sandwiches for 10 minutes or until golden and flat. Another option is to place the sandwiches into a large cast iron skillet and place another on top to press, or you can simply put them into a sandwich press. Either method will require around the same amount of time. Whatever method you choose, serve the sandwich by slicing diagonally and then plating while hot.

Product Yield

This recipe for The Third Dimension Cuban Sandwich produces 4 servings. Dose strength per serving will be determined by what you choose from the dosing chart. If you want a lighter dose and lighter serving you can cut the sandwiches into 8 servings.

American Yumboldt Chicken Club Sandwich

The Club sandwich was supposedly invented in Saratoga Springs, New York during the late 19th century. This sandwich is also known as the "clubhouse sandwich" and "double-decker." The pine and skunky undertones of Yumboldt bring the missing element to this sandwich making for a delightful lunch.

Directions

Toast the apple bread slices then lay out onto a flat surface like a cutting board. Mix 4 servings of dosed decarboxylated Yumboldt Kief into the guacamole and then divide into 4 servings or 2 tablespoons each.

Starting with one sandwich, lay out 3 pieces of toasted bread on a cutting board in a row. Take 1 serving of dosed guacamole and spread onto the top and bottom piece of bread leaving the middle slice plain. Lay down 3 slices of deli chicken

Mise en place

- 12 slices deli chicken breast
- 12 slices cooked apple bacon
- 12 slices apple bread
- 8 tablespoons non-medicated guacamole
- 4 servings of dosed decarboxylated Yumboldt Kief*
- 1 large tomato
- 1 cup spring salad mix

* Add the desired dose of decarboxylated Yumboldt kief or alternative decarboxylated strain kief into this dish per serving by referring to the dosing chart on page 15 and decarboxylation process on page 16.

Dietary Lifestyle

O

breast on the bottom piece of bread or the one closest to you. Take the plain middle slice of bread and place it on top of the deli chicken breast.

Divide the spring salad mix into 4 servings or ¼ cup each. Place ¼ cup of this spring mix on top of the toasted plain bread, followed by 3 strips of bacon and 2 slices of tomatoes. Close the sandwich and gently press down to glue your sandwich together. Repeat for the other 3 sandwiches. Slice diagonally with a pickle or chips to serve.

Product Yield

This recipe for American Yumboldt Chicken Club Sandwich produces 4 servings. Dose strength per serving will be determined by what you choose from the dosing chart.

Polish Open Face Cheesus Sandwich

Open face sandwiches are a popular street food in Poland and are known as "zapiekanki." These sandwiches are traditionally garnished with ketchup, but I find that tomato paste is a healthier option. Cheesus adds a wonderful array of flavors that enhance the earthiness of the mushrooms and uplift the cheesiness of the shredded cheese. It also brightens the tomato paste with a slight sweetness and tartness, which leaves your taste buds wanting more.

Directions

Dice the onions and place in a non-stick pan with the mushrooms and sauté until translucent. Pull from the stove and set aside. In a bowl, place the tomato paste,

Mise en place

12 slices roast beef

2 small loaves of French bread or any bread baguette of your choice

2 sweet Vidalia onions

2 cups shredded mozzarella cheese

1 carton button mushrooms

1 small can tomato paste

4 tablespoons Clarified Herbed Cheesus Cannabutter*

* Follow the recipe for Clarified Herbed Cannabutter on page 29 and add the desired dose of Cheesus or alternative strain by referring to the dosing chart on page 15.

Dietary Lifestyle

O

and then fill the can with water to add to the paste. Stir the water and tomato paste until it creates a thick sauce then set aside.

Slice the two loves of bread lengthwise through the middle to create 4 halves and place on a sheet pan. Spread 1 tablespoon of Clarified Herbed Cheesus Cannabutter onto each slice making sure to evenly cover the bread. Now add 3 slices of roast beef per slice then spread your vegetable mixture evenly between all of the slices. Next add ½ cup of shredded mozzarella cheese per slice then drizzle your tomato sauce mixture over the top of the cheese.

Turn your oven to broil and place the open face sandwiches under the broiler for 8 to 10 minutes, or until the cheese melts and the bread becomes slightly browned around the edges.

Product Yield

This recipe for Polish Open Face Cheesus Sandwich produces 4 servings. Dose strength per serving will be determined by what you choose from the dosing chart. If you want a lighter dose and lighter serving you can cut the sandwiches into 8 servings.

English Cucumber Speed Queen Sandwich

Mise en place

8 slices white bread

1 small cucumber

4 tablespoons cream cheese

4 tablespoons Clarified Herbed
   Speed Queen Cannabutter*

Sea salt and pepper to taste

The traditional English cucumber sandwich is of British origin and was held in high esteem by the rich in the Victorian Era. This sandwich was served at afternoon tea and was a sandwich of leisure of the upper class. English cucumber sandwiches are still being served today but now they are enjoyed by all. Speed Queen embodies fruity, citrus, floral, mint and Skunk flavors which pair wonderfully with the creaminess of the cream cheese, starchiness of the bread, richness of the cannabutter and the refreshing coolness of the cucumbers.

Directions

In a small ramekin, stir the cream cheese and Clarified Herbed Speed Queen Cannabutter until fully mixed. Spread 2 tablespoons of this mixture onto 2 halves of bread and repeat for the other slices. Slice your cucumber either ultra-thin for a delicate sandwich or medium thickness for a more filling sandwich. Season the slices lightly with sea salt and pepper.

Take two slices of bread and lay the cucumbers on one side only, then press together. Repeat this process until you have 4 sandwiches total. Then take a knife and carefully cut off all the crusts from the sandwiches and slice diagonally. Serve with English Breakfast tea or any tea of your choice.

Product Yield

This recipe for English Cucumber Speed Queen Sandwiches produces 4 servings. Your dose per serving will depend on the medication strength you pick from the dosing chart.

* Follow the recipe for Clarified Herbed Cannabutter on page 29 and add the desired dose of Speed Queen or alternative strain by referring to the dosing chart on page 15.

Dietary Lifestyle

O, OLV, LV, P

SECTION FOUR

Appetizers

American Herbed Blue Cheese Biscuits
Vietnamese Lemon Kush Kief Spring Rolls
Middle Eastern Afghan Kush Hummus
Super Lemon Haze Mexican Guacamole
American Carnival Baked Sweet Potato Fries
French ABV Brie En Croûte
Algerian Skunk #1 Salad
East African Spice Pea Soup
Mediterranean ABV Goat Cheese Spread
Central Italian Lemon Skunk Bruschetta

American Herbed Blue Cheese Biscuits

Biscuits were originally created in the early days to be used as a nutritious food that was easy to store on long journeys. These biscuits were usually baked in such a way as to produce a hard and long lasting texture, which would ensure longevity. Influenced by European settlers, American biscuits are softer and very similar to a savory European scone. The strain Blue Cheese adds a savoury, cheese-like taste that rounds out the actual taste of these American herbed biscuits.

Directions

In a large bowl, sift together the all-purpose flour, wheat flour, baking powder and baking soda. Then add the basil, marjoram, Italian seasoning, sun dried tomatoes,

Mise en place

6 servings of dosed decarboxylated
  Blue Cheese*

1 cup all-purpose flour

1 cup wheat flour

1 cup blue cheese crumbles

¾ cup sour cream

⅓ cup smoked sun dried tomatoes

¼ cup milk

4 tablespoons butter

2 teaspoons baking powder

1 tablespoon fresh minced basil

1 tablespoon fresh minced marjoram

1 teaspoon dried Italian seasoning

½ teaspoon baking soda

Cracked sea salt to garnish

* Add the desired dose of decarboxylated Blue Cheese or alternative decarboxylated strain into this dish per serving by referring to the dosing chart on page 15 and decarboxylation process on page 16.

Dietary Lifestyle
O, OLV, LV, P

Appetizers

blue cheese, milk, sour cream and butter. Grind up the dosed decarboxylated Blue Cheese cannabis and add to the bowl. Stir the ingredients until well incorporated and form into a sticky dough.

Preheat your oven to 375°F. Flour a cutting board and then place the dough on top of the flour. Sprinkle some more flour on top of the dough and then roll out. Using a biscuit or pastry cutter, cut 12 servings out of the dough and sparsely season with sea salt. You do not want to over season with sea salt due to the blue cheese being salty. You are merely looking for texture, and mouth feel with a light contrast of flavor. Place the biscuits onto a non-stick sheet pan and bake for 12 to 15 minutes or until goldon brown.

Product Yield

This recipe for American Herbed Blue Cheese Biscuits produces 12 servings. Dose strength per serving will be determined by what you choose from the dosing chart. Remember, this is merely an appetizer and is intended to be a light dose of cannabis in case you plan to follow up with another medicated dish.

Vietnamese Lemon Kush Kief Spring Rolls

Mise en place

16 small sprigs Thai basil

16 mint leaves

8 rice wrappers

8 servings of dosed decarboxylated
    Lemon Kush kief*

1 avocado

2 cups chopped lettuce mix of your
    choice

½ cup shredded carrot

4 ounces vermicelli noodles

Spring rolls or "Goi cuon" are commonly known as "summer rolls" in Vietnam. These rolls can be filled with a variety of fresh ingredients that reflect the freshness of the spring and summer months. Lemon Kush's lemony taste with floral and mint undertones deepens the flavors in this dish because of the similar taste profiles in the food items. Enjoy as an appetizer or even as a light meal.

Directions

In a medium sized ramekin, mix all of the ingredients listed under the dipping sauce section until well combined. Cover, then set aside to let the flavors deepen.

Soak the vermicelli noodles in hot water until fully soft or according to directions on the package. Drain, divide into 8 small portions and set aside. Then soak the

* Add the desired dose of decarboxylated Lemon Kush kief or alternative decarboxylated strain kief into this dish per serving by referring to the dosing chart on page 15 and decarboxylation process on page 16.

Dietary Lifestyle

O, GF (both spring rolls and sauce. But make sure the sweet red chili sauce and fish sauce are labeled GF)
OLV, OV, LV, P, V (only the spring rolls)

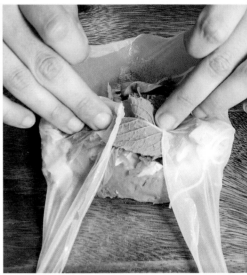
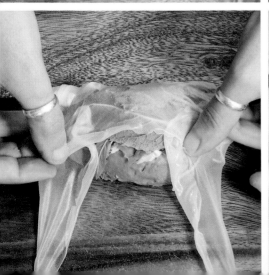

Appetizers

rice papers in hot water until fully soft or according to directions on the package. Place one portion of vermicelli noodles down near one edge of the first rice paper, leaving a little room. Slice the avocado into 8 pieces and place 1 piece on top of the vermicelli noodle.

Divide the chopped lettuce mix into 8 portions or ¼ cup each. Spread 1 portion of chopped lettuce mixture onto the avocado. Divide the shredded carrot into 8 portions or 1 tablespoon each. Spread 1 portion of the shredded carrot on top of the chopped lettuce mixture. Place 2 sprigs of Thai basil on top of the shredded carrot follow by 2 mint leaves.

Take 1 dose of dosed decarboxylated Lemon Kush kief and divide it in to 2. Sprinkle ½ of the dosed decarboxylated Lemon Kush kief and save the other ½ for the next spring roll. Remember, there will be 4 servings with 2 spring rolls per serving. Flip both sides of the rice paper inwards so that they meet over the middle of the noodle pile, then roll from the bottom of the spring roll forward to encase the filling. Plate with the dipping sauce and serve.

Even though this is an appetizer dish, it is designed for a full dose per serving due to its versatility in being potentially used for a light lunch or light dinner dish. If you plan on making a medicated dish to follow these spring rolls as appetizers you can lower the medication by cutting each dose in half.

Product Yield

This recipe for Vietnamese Lemon Kush Kief Spring Rolls produces 4 servings with 2 spring rolls per serving. Dose strength per serving will be determined by what you choose from the dosing chart.

Mise en place
Dipping Sauce
1 clove garlic minced
2 tablespoons crushed peanuts
1 tablespoon water
1 tablespoon lime juice
6 teaspoons sweet red chili sauce
1 tablespoon turbinado sugar
1 teaspoon fish sauce

Middle Eastern Afghan Kush Hummus

Hummus is a popular food throughout the Middle East, and is a staple food and a part of most everyday meals. The sweet citrus with mild Skunk undertones of Afghan Kush really support and expand the Middle Eastern flavors in this dish. Pair with some fresh pita and it will be hard to eat just one serving of this delicious edible.

Directions

In a food processor, add the chickpeas, lemon juice, Basic Afghan Kush Olive Oil, garlic, tahini paste, paprika, cumin and sea salt. Process this mixture until it achieves the creaminess you desire. The longer you process this mixture the smoother it will become. Garnish with a few pinches of paprika and drizzle non-medicated olive oil on top to serve.

Product Yield

This recipe for Middle Eastern Afghan Kush Hummus produces 4 servings. Dose strength per serving will be determined by what you choose from the dosing chart. Remember, this is merely an appetizer and is intended to be a light dose of cannabis in case you plan to follow up with another medicated dish.

Mise en place

2 cups chickpeas

4 tablespoons lemon juice

4 tablespoons Basic Afghan Kush Olive Oil*

4 cloves garlic

2 tablespoons tahini paste

1 teaspoon paprika

1 teaspoon cumin

¼ teaspoon sea salt

* Follow the recipe for Basic Olive Oil on page 35 and add the desired dose of Afghan Kush or alternative strain by referring to the dosing chart on page 15.

Dietary Lifestyle

O, OLV, OV, LV, P, V, GF

Super Lemon Haze Mexican Guacamole

Mise en place

4 Haas avocados

1 sweet white onion

2 small heads of garlic

1 cup small cherry tomatoes

1 lime

1 fluid ounce of Basic Super Lemon
   Haze Olive Oil*

1 level teaspoon paprika

1 level teaspoon chili powder

½ level teaspoon cayenne pepper

Cracked pepper and sea salt to taste

In the early 16th century, guacamole was made by the Aztecs in central Mexico. The candied lemon and sweet floral notes of the Super Lemon Haze balance out the acidity of the guacamole, creating a match made in heaven. This guacamole can be used by itself or in a variety of other dishes as a condiment.

Directions

Remove the skins and seeds from the avocados then mash them in a medium sized bowl. Dice the onion, cherry tomatoes and garlic then add to the bowl. Cut the lime in ½ then squeeze the juice of both halves onto this mixture. Add the Basic Super Lemon Haze Olive Oil, paprika, chili powder, cayenne pepper, cracked pepper and sea salt. Stir this mixture until fully combined and check to see if you need to season with a little more cracked pepper and sea salt. Chill for 30 minutes before serving for a cool treat or even serve at room temperature.

Product Yield

This recipe for Super Lemon Haze Mexican Guacamole produces 4 servings. Remember, this is merely an appetizer and is intended to be a light dose of cannabis in case you plan to follow up with another medicated dish.

* Follow the recipe for Basic Olive Oil on page 35 and add the desired dose of Super Lemon Haze or alternative strain by referring to the dosing chart on page 15.

Dietary Lifestyle

O, OLV, OV, LV, P, V, GF

Appetizers

American Carnival Baked Sweet Potato Fries

Sweet potato fries are a popular way to cook sweet potatoes in North America. In some parts of North America these fries are served with melted butter and honey on top of them. When I was younger, this was one of my favorite treats to enjoy during the summer months down by the boat harbor. The sugary lemon and hints of mixed citrus in the Carnival strain really make the dipping sauce in this dish pop, thus creating the perfect accompaniment to the fries.

Directions

Preheat your oven to 450°F. Cut your sweet potatoes into fries by hand or with a French fry cutter. You can choose the thickness of the fry to your own personal liking, but if you end up making steak fries make sure to increase the cooking time.

Pour the olive oil in a bowl and toss the sweet potato fries in it until evenly coated. Lay your fries onto a baking sheet then bake for 20 minutes or until browned and crisp. While your fries are baking divide the raw honey into 4 servings or ¼ cup each. To each serving of honey add 1 tablespoon Clarified Carnival Cannabutter and 1 teaspoon cinnamon in a ramekin. Combine all ingredients by stirring fast until fully incorporated.

Once your fries are done baking, season with sea salt and pepper. Plate your fries with the cinnamon-honey cannabutter dipping sauce to serve. You can also make this a low dose appetizer in case you plan to follow up with another medicated dish. To do this, simply cut the Clarified Carnival Cannabutter by half in each serving.

Product Yield

This recipe for American Carnival Baked Sweet Potato Fries produces 4 servings. Dose strength per serving will be determined by what you choose from the dosing chart.

Mise en place

4 medium sweet potatoes or 2 extra-large sweet potatoes

1 cup raw honey

4 teaspoons cinnamon

4 tablespoons room temperature Basic Clarified Carnival Cannabutter*

2 to 3 tablespoons olive oil

Sea salt and pepper to taste

*Follow the recipe for Basic Clarified Cannabutter on page 27 and add the desired dose of Carnival or alternative strain by referring to the dosing chart on page 15.

Dietary Lifestyle

O, OLV, LV, P, GF

French ABV Brie en Croûte

The French phrase "en croûte" translates to "in a crust," and in French cuisine this term is applied to any food item that is wrapped in pastry dough and then baked in the oven. The syrupy sweet floral notes of the ABV cannabis pair wonderfully with the buttery flavors of the cheese and pastry. This is an elegant dish that will be sure to impress any dinner guest when served as an appetizer before the main course.

Directions

Preheat your oven to 375°F. Unfold and lay the puff pastry sheet flat onto your cutting board or workspace. Take your brie wheel with the rind intact and place in the center of the puff pastry sheet. Spread the blackberry jam on top of the cheese

Mise en place

8 ounce brie wheel

4 servings of dosed ABV cannabis*

1 sheet puff pastry

1 egg

⅓ cup blackberry jam

¼ cup sliced raw almonds

* Add the desired dose ABV (already been vaped) cannabis by referring to the dosing chart on page 15.

Dietary Lifestyle

O, OLV, P

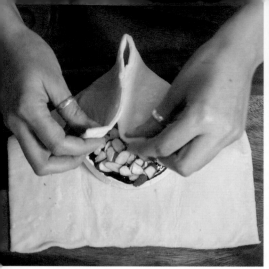

wheel until the top is fully and evenly covered. Sprinkle the ABV cannabis on top of the jam followed by the sliced almonds.

Fold each corner of the puff pastry towards the center until the entire cheese wheel is sealed by the pastry sheet. Crack the egg open into a small ramekin and beat with a fork. Spread or brush the egg mixture over the top and the sides of the puff pastry dough. Place your Brie en Croûte on an ungreased cooking sheet and bake for 15 to 20 minutes or until golden brown and puffed.

Product Yield

This recipe for French ABV Brie en Croûte will produce 8 servings. Your dose per serving will depend on the medication strength you pick from the dosing chart. Remember, this is merely an appetizer and is intended to be a light dose of cannabis in case you plan to follow up with another medicated dish.

Algerian Skunk #1 Salad

Algerian salads are very diverse and can use a number of combinations of fresh vegetables, making this dish a perfect start before a main course. The Skunk #1 lends a sweet Skunk flavor with minimal hash and fruit undertones which add to the cultural flavoring of this dish.

Directions

Coarsely chop the peppers, onion, cucumber, tomato and fresh mint leaves. Place these ingredients into a bowl to be dressed. Slice the black olives in half then add into the vegetable mixture. Drop the coriander into the bowl followed by the Skunk #1 Basic Olive Oil and balsamic vinegar. Fold this mixture until the vegetables are saturated in the dressing. Now slice the 2 hardboiled eggs to 3 sections each to produce 6 slices. Spoon this mixture onto 4 appetizer plates then garnish with 2 egg slices and some fresh whole mint leaves.

Product Yield

This recipe for Algerian Skunk # 1 Salad produces 4 servings. Your dose per serving will depend on the medication strength you pick from the dosing chart. This dose will then be further divided by 4 to produce a lower cannabis dose. Remember, this is merely an appetizer and is intended to be a light dose of cannabis in case you plan to follow up with another medicated dish.

Mise en place

2 hardboiled eggs
1 green sweet bell pepper
1 red sweet bell pepper
1 sweet Vidalia onion
1 cucumber
1 tomato
½ cup pitted black olives
½ cup fresh mint leaves
1 fluid ounce Basic Skunk #1 Olive Oil*
2 tablespoons balsamic vinegar**
1 teaspoon crushed coriander
Sea salt and pepper to taste

* Follow the recipe for Basic Olive Oil on page 35 and add the desired dose of Skunk #1 or alternative strain by referring to the dosing chart on page 15
** If you do not like balsamic vinegar you can use red wine vinegar or any other vinegar of your choice.

Dietary Lifestyle

O, OLV, OV, P, GF

East African Spice Pea Soup

Many delicious soups come out of east Africa, all filled with savory flavors and spices sure to please many palates. The hash and sandalwood flavors of the Spice strain really lend another dimension of taste that enhances the spices in this dish. This dish will certainly warm the body and soul with its medley of flavors.

Directions

Place the Basic Clarified Spice Cannabutter, onion, garlic and sweet potato into a stockpot and sauté until the onions become translucent. Now add in the coriander, cardamom, cumin, ginger, cayenne pepper, sea salt, and black pepper. Let this mixture infuse on medium heat for 5 minutes while stirring. Add the 3 cups of

Mise en place

3 cups peas

3 cups water

1 cup chopped onion

1 chopped sweet potato

1 fresh tomato or cherry tomatoes to garnish

3 tablespoons Basic Clarified Spice Cannabutter*

2 tablespoons minced garlic

1 teaspoon coriander

1 teaspoon cardamom

1 teaspoon cumin

1 teaspoon ginger

1 teaspoon sea salt

½ teaspoon black pepper

¼ teaspoon cayenne pepper

* Follow the recipe for Basic Clarified Cannabutter on page 27 and add the desired dose of Spice or alternative strain by referring to the dosing chart on page 15.

Dietary Lifestyle

O, OLV, LV, P, GF

water and 2 cups of peas then cover the stockpot. Bring this mixture to a boil for 8 minutes then drop down to a simmer.

Let this mixture simmer for 30 minutes then pull from the stove and pour into a blender. Emulsify the mixture with the blender then pour it back into the stockpot. Add the last cup of peas and let the peas warm up in the soup mixture for 5 minutes on medium low. Pour into serving bowls then garnish with fresh tomato slices and fresh herbs.

Product Yield

This recipe for East African Spice Pea Soup produces 6 servings. Remember, this is merely an appetizer and is intended to be a light dose of cannabis in case you plan to follow up with another medicated dish.

Appetizers

Mediterranean ABV Goat Cheese Spread

Goat cheese has been produced for over thousands of years in all areas of the world. It gained popularity all over the Mediterranean area because it was a cheese that could be stored in areas where refrigeration was limited or non-existent. The sweet floral tones of ABV cannabis really help to balance the acidity of the cheese. This creates the perfect backdrop to the additional ingredients that are found in this appetizer.

Directions

In a small mixing bowl, combine the goat cheese, orange zest, cayenne pepper, paprika, halved raw walnuts, wild honey and dosed ABV cannabis. Stir this mixture until creamy and all of the ingredients are fully incorporated. You can chill this mixture for a firmer cheese or leave at room temperature for a silkier mouth feel. Spread this mixture onto mini crackers of your choice and serve as an appetizer.

Product Yield

This recipe creates 1¾ cup of Mediterranean ABV Goat Cheese Spread. Remember, this is merely an appetizer and is intended to be a light dose of cannabis in case you plan to follow up with another medicated dish.

Mise en place

8 ounces goat cheese (chèvre)
4 servings of dosed ABV cannabis*
The zest of 1 orange
½ cup halved raw walnuts
¼ cup wild honey
⅛ teaspoon cayenne pepper
⅛ teaspoon paprika

* Add the desired dose of the ABV (already been vaped) cannabis by referring to the dosing chart on page 15.

Dietary Lifestyle

O, OLV, LV, P

Central Italian Lemon Skunk Bruschetta

Mise en place

6 plum tomatoes

8 fresh basil leaves

3 medium sized fresh Mozzarella balls

3 cloves garlic

1 shallot

1 fresh small baguette

1 fluid ounce Basic Lemon Skunk
  Olive Oil*

1 tablespoon balsamic vinegar

Sea salt and pepper to taste

Bruschetta is a traditional antipasto in Italy that dates back to the 15th century. Antipasto means "before the meal" and is generally part of a series of courses in the traditional Italian meal. Lemon Skunk offers a citrus flavor with bold Skunk and fruit tones, which really enhance all the components of this dish.

Directions

Coarsely chop the tomatoes, basil leaves, mozzarella balls, garlic, and shallot. Gather all the coarsely chopped ingredients into a bowl and add the Basic Lemon Skunk Basic Olive Oil. Then add the balsamic vinegar, sea salt and pepper. Toss the mixture until well lubricated by the oil and balsamic vinegar.

Slice the fresh baguette widthwise and lay the slices in an ungreased pan. Put the pan under your broiler in the oven for 5 minutes or until slightly golden brown and crispy. Pull from the oven and spoon your tomato mixture onto the pieces of bread while the bread is warm. Divide the slices of bruschetta into 4 servings and serve.

Product Yield

This recipe for Central Italian Lemon Skunk Bruschetta produces 4 servings. Your dose per serving will depend on the medication strength you pick from the dosing chart. Remember, this is merely an appetizer and is intended to be a light dose of cannabis in case you plan to follow up with another medicated dish.

* Follow the recipe for Basic Olive Oil on page 35 and add the desired dose of Lemon Skunk or alternative strain by referring to the dosing chart on page 15.

Dietary Lifestyle

O, OLV, LV, P

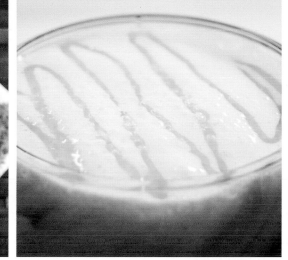

Drinks

Mexican Hash Plant Chocolate

Shiva's Indian Spiced Butter Chai

Vietnamese Mako Haze Iced Coffee

Australian Milo Banana Kush Smoothie

Indian Mango Lassi

American DJ Short's Blueberry Vanilla
Protein Shake

Vietnamese Ultra Skunk Avocado Smoothie

American Strawberry Cough Milkshake

Puerto Rican Pineapple Kush Piña Colada

Spanish Orange Kush Sangria

Mexican Hash Plant Chocolate

The first form of drinking chocolate was created by the Mayans over 2,000 years ago and was actually served cold. By the 15th century the Aztecs began to take over areas that the Mayans resided in and adopted this chocolate drink into their culture. It wasn't until later that this chocolate drink would be served warm and sweeter than its original version. The heavy earth and hash notes of the Hash Plant strain adds a depth of flavor that cannot be matched when compared to un-medicated Mexican Hot Chocolate. Brilliant and complex, this drink will take your taste buds on a trip through the past.

Directions

In a saucepan on the stove place the Mexican chocolate, whole milk, cinnamon sticks, vanilla bean, sugar, ancho chili powder and sea salt. Bring this mixture up to a simmer on medium low and stir every few minutes for 12 minutes for a uniform drink. When the 12 minutes are up pull from the stove then stir in the decarboxylated Hash Plant kief and pour into mugs. Sprinkle with a little more ancho chili powder and a cinnamon stick to garnish.

Product Yield

This recipe for Hash Plant Mexican Hot Chocolate produces a 16oz drink. Dose strength per serving will be determined by what you choose from the dosing chart.

Mise en place

4 ounces chopped Mexican Chocolate

2 cups whole milk

2 cinnamon sticks

1 vanilla bean split length wise down the middle

2 tablespoons turbinado sugar

¼ teaspoon ancho chili powder

1 pinch sea salt

1 serving of dosed decarboxylated Hash Plant kief*

* Add the desired dose of decarboxylated Hash Plant kief or alternative decarboxylated strain kief by referring to the dosing chart on page 15 and decarboxylation process on page 16.

Dietary Lifestyle

O, OLV, LV, P, GF (make sure the Mexican chocolate is pure and not cut with any fillers and labeled as GF)

Shiva's Indian Spiced Butter Chai

Chai is a generic word for "tea" and masala chai means "spiced tea." Spiced chai originates in India where it is flavored with complex herbs and spices. There is no set recipe or steps that must be followed for spiced chai as there are many different versions passed down through families. The sweet Skunk and earthy pine tones really fit well with the herb and spice mixture in this drink.

Directions for the strainer method

On your stovetop, turn the burner on medium and let it heat up for approximately 5 minutes. Keep the stovetop on the medium setting and place a small saucepan on the burner. Combine all of the ingredients in the pan and cook this mixture for 5 minutes.

Remove this mixture from the stove and pour through a fine mesh strainer into your desired cup. Very gently use a spoon to push against the tea and spice mixture

Mise en place

1 cup whole milk

1 cup water

2 teaspoons loose leaf black tea

1 teaspoon of Basic Clarified Shiva Cannabutter*

1 to 3 teaspoons turbinado sugar to taste

½ teaspoon vanilla extract

⅛ teaspoon cardamom

⅛ teaspoon cinnamon for the tea bag method or ½ stick of cinnamon for the strainer method

⅛ teaspoon cloves

⅛ teaspoon ginger

*Follow the recipe for Basic Clarified Cannabutter on page 27 and add the desired dose of Shiva or alternative strain by referring to the dosing chart on page 15.

Dietary Lifestyle

O, OLV, LV, P, GF

to release any fluid it may be holding. Discard this mixture of herbal material as this is not something you want to consume by itself nor reuse.

Directions for the homemade tea bag method

Go to your local organic market or specialty tea shop to find fillable tea bags for your own blend of tea. Generally you can buy a box of these pre-made empty tea bags or you can buy single, reusable ones. Either will work and both are perfectly fine for this recipe.

Fill one bag with the tea and spices then close the tea bag. Set your bag aside and choose from the following two methods on how to prepare your tea

Method 1

Heat the water in a kettle or saucepan until it starts to boil then take it off the stove. Pour the boiling water into a cup then add the tea bag and Basic Clarified Shiva Cannabutter. Let the tea bag steep for 5 minutes and then add in your milk and vanilla extract. At this point you can take your tea bag out or continue to let it steep as you drink it for a stronger flavor.

Method 2

Place the water, milk, Basic Clarified Shiva Cannabutter and tea bag in a cup. Place in the microwave and cook for 1 minute and 30 seconds. Pull from the microwave to add the sugar and vanilla extract. Place in the microwave for another 30 seconds to finish.

Product Yield

This recipe for Shiva's Indian Spiced Butter Chai produces a 16 oz drink. Dose strength per serving will be determined by what you choose from the dosing chart.

Vietnamese Caramella Iced Coffee

Mise en place

8 ice cubes

1 cup dark roast coffee

¼ cup sweetened condensed milk

1 teaspoon Madagascar Vanilla Bean
   Caramella Bourbon Extract

Directions

Combine the sweetened condensed milk and Madagascar Vanilla Bean Caramella Bourbon Extract together then pour into the bottom of the glass. Add the ice cubes into the glass and pour the hot dark roast coffee over the ice and medicated condensed milk mixture. Serve with a spoon to stir or scoop up the sweet bottom as you drink.

Product Yield

This recipe produces one serving of Vietnamese Caramella Iced Coffee but can be doubled to produce two drinks. Dose strength per serving will be determined by what you choose from the dosing chart.

* Add the desired dose of the Caramella strain or alternative strain into your Madagascar Vanilla Bean Bourbon Extract by referring to the dosing chart on page 16 and the Madagascar Vanilla Bean Bourbon Extract recipe on page 45.

Dietary Lifestyle

O, OLV, LV, P, GF

Australian Milo Banana Kush Smoothie

Mise en place

Milo powder was originally created in Sydney, Australia in 1934 by Australian chemist and inventor, Thomas Mayne. Milo drinks are traditionally served in Australia either hot or cold. Banana Kush imparts a strong, sweet banana taste that boosts the banana flavor in this smoothie.

Directions

In a blender, combine all of the ingredients until smooth and uniform. Serve this drink immediately and pour into a chilled glass for an extra cold treat in the warmer months.

Product Yield

This recipe for Australian Milo Banana Kush Smoothie produces 1 drink but can be doubled to produce 2 drinks. Dose strength per serving will be determined by what you choose from the dosing chart.

5 to 8 ice cubes

2 bananas

½ cup milk

2 tablespoons Milo or other chocolate malt powder

1½ tablespoons vanilla flavored yogurt

1 tablespoon Banana Kush Raw Coconut Honey*

* Follow the recipe for Raw Coconut Honey on page 41 and add the desired dose of Banana Kush or alternative strain by referring to the dosing chart on page 15.

Dietary Lifestyle

O, OLV, LV, P

Indian Mango Lassi

Lassis are very traditional and popular yogurt drinks in India and they come in a wide array of flavors. The Mango strain deepens and sweetens the already present mango flavor in this drink. This is a great drink to be enjoyed at any time of the day, during the warmer months or paired with your favorite Indian dish.

Directions

In a blender, add the ice cubes, yogurt, milk, diced mango, Mango Raw Coconut Honey and cardamom powder. Blend this mixture on high until it reaches a smooth and homogenized texture. Drizzle clover honey on top and serve immediately.

Product Yield

This recipe for Indian Mango Lassi produces 1 drink but can be doubled to produce 2 drinks. Dose strength per serving will be determined by what you choose from the dosing chart.

Mise en place

8 ice cubes

1 cup plain yogurt

1 cup diced ripe mango

⅛ cup milk

1 tablespoon Mango Raw Coconut
　Honey*

⅛ teaspoon cardamom powder

Non-medicated clover honey reserve

*Follow the recipe for Raw Coconut Honey on page 41 and add the desired dose of Mango or alternative strain by referring to the dosing chart on page 15.

Dietary Lifestyle

O, OLV, LV, P, GF

American DJ Short's Blueberry Vanilla Protein Shake

Protein powders have become a staple in the fitness and health world of America. Coming from a variety of different sources these protein powders are great for the body due to their dense form of nutrients. DJ Short's Blueberry lends a sweet blueberry taste that uplifts the blueberries in this shake. This shake will be a great addition to your pre-workout or post-workout nutrition plan.

Directions

Place all the ingredients in a blender and blend this mixture on high until it reaches a uniform consistency. Consume this beverage within 30 minutes of finishing your workout.

Product Yield

This recipe for DJ Short's Blueberry Vanilla Protein Shake produces 1 drink but can be doubled to produce 2 drinks. Dose strength per serving will be determined by what you choose from the dosing chart.

Mise en place

8 ice cubes

2 bananas

2 scoops vanilla protein powder of your choice

1 scoop creatine powder

½ cup frozen blueberries

½ cup vanilla yogurt

½ cup water

1 tablespoon DJ Short's Blueberry Raw Coconut Honey*

* Follow the recipe for Raw Coconut Honey on page 41 and add the desired dose of DJ Short's Blueberry or alternative strain by referring to the dosing chart on page 15.

Dietary Lifestyle

O, OLV, LV, P, GF

Vietnamese Ultra Skunk Avocado Smoothie

Mise en place

1 ripe avocado

8 ice cubes

½ cup milk

⅓ cup sweetened condensed milk

2 tablespoons Ultra Skunk Raw
   Coconut Honey*

In Vietnam, avocado smoothies known as "sinh to bo" are a traditional drink that are served at any time of the day and with any kind of meal. The Ultra Skunk in this recipe with its fruity Skunk and floral tones paired with condensed milk amplify the flavor of the avocado. Enjoy when you are in need of an exotic treat that is less than ordinary.

Directions

Place the ice cubes, milk, sweetened condensed milk and Ultra Skunk Raw Coconut Honey in a blender. Cut the avocado lengthwise then seed it. Scoop out the flesh and add to the blender. Blend this mixture on high until it reaches a smooth and uniform texture. Serve immediately.

Product Yield

This recipe for Vietnamese Ultra Skunk Avocado Smoothie produces 1 drink but can be doubled to produce 2 drinks. Dose strength per serving will be determined by what you choose from the dosing chart.

*Follow the recipe for Raw Coconut Honey on page 41 and add the desired dose of Ultra Skunk or alternative strain by referring to the dosing chart on page 15.

Dietary Lifestyle

O, OLV, LV, P, GF

American Strawberry Cough Milkshake

Mise en place

- I cup fresh strawberries
- ¾ cup whole milk
- 1 pint vanilla bean ice cream
- 2 tablespoons sugar
- 1 tablespoon malt powder (optional)
- 2 teaspoons Strawberry Cough Madagascar Vanilla Bean Bourbon Extract*

Milkshakes were created in America in 1885, but rather than the milkshakes we know today they were tonics using whiskey that were very similar to eggnog. By the 1900s, people began to take out the whiskey and use different flavored syrups, followed closely by ice cream. The sugary strawberries and cream profile of Strawberry Cough intensifies the strawberry-cream flavors present in this milkshake. Enjoy on a hot summer day, with your favorite burger or even as a dessert.

Directions

Place the strawberries, milk, ice cream, sugar, Strawberry Cough Madagascar Vanilla Bean Bourbon Extract and malt powder (if using) in a blender. Blend until the mixture turns into a uniform creamy milkshake. Garnish with fresh strawberries and serve immediately.

Product Yield

This recipe for American Strawberry Cough Milkshake produces 2 drinks but the recipe can be cut in half to produce 1 drink. Dose strength per serving will be determined by what you choose from the dosing chart.

* Follow the recipe for Madagascar Vanilla Bean Bourbon Extract on page 45 and add the desired dose of Strawberry Cough or alternative strain by referring to the dosing chart on page 15.

Dietary Lifestyle

O, OLV, LV, P, GF (make sure the ice cream has no fillers and the label reads GF. Exclude the malt in this recipe for GF)

Puerto Rican Pineapple Kush Piña Colada

The piña colada was created in 1954 by Ramon Marrero and has been the official drink of Puerto Rico since 1978. Pineapple Kush adds tart and fruity pineapple tones that magnify the already existent pineapple flavor in this drink. This is a great drink to enjoy during the hot summer months when you want to relax and cool off.

Directions

Place all of the ingredients in a blender and blend on high. You can adjust the sweetness by using more or less of the turbinado sugar. Although this drink already contains the bourbon extract you can spice it up by adding in 1 fluid ounce of rum. Pour into a chilled glass and serve immediately.

Product Yield

This recipe for Cuban Pineapple Kush Piña Colada produces 1 drink but can be doubled to produce 2 drinks. Dose strength per serving will be determined by what you choose from the dosing chart.

Mise en place

- 1 cup small ice cubes
- 4 fluid ounces coconut milk
- 6 tablespoons crushed sweetened pineapple
- 2 fluid ounces pineapple juice
- 1-2 tablespoon turbinado sugar
- 1 teaspoon Pineapple Kush Madagascar Vanilla Bean Bourbon Extract*

*Follow the recipe for Madagascar Vanilla Bean Bourbon Extract on page 45 and add the desired dose of Pineapple Kush or alternative strain by referring to the dosing chart on page 15.

Dietary Lifestyle

O, OLV, OV, LV, P, GF

Spanish Orange Kush Sangria

Sangria is served through Spain during the summer months and has many variations depending on what area of Spain it comes from. The Orange Kush in this recipe provides sweet orange and citrus notes that boost all flavor components of this drink. Sangria is a great social drink that can be served at gatherings and is sure to be a crowd pleaser, or you can simply enjoy the luxury of this drink by yourself.

Directions

Pour the whole bottle of Shiraz into a glass pitcher then squeeze the juices of 1 orange and 1 lemon into the red wine. You can place a strainer under the fruit to catch the seeds or the pulp, if you like. Discard the squeezed orange and lemon or save them to boil on your stove to deodorize your kitchen.

Cut the remaining lemon and orange into slices and add them into the pitcher. Now add in your Orange Kush Madagascar Vanilla Bean Bourbon Extract and sugar then stir until incorporated. Place the pitcher in the fridge overnight for the flavors to

Mise en place

1 bottle Shiraz

2 large oranges

2 large lemons

2½ cups club soda

6 teaspoons Orange Kush Madagascar Vanilla Bean Bourbon Extract*

¼ cup turbinado sugar

*Follow the recipe for Madagascar Vanilla Bean Bourbon Extract on page 45 and add the desired dose of Orange Kush or alternative strain by referring to the dosing chart on page 15.

Dietary Lifestyle

O, OLV, OV, LV, P, GF

deepen and develop. Pull from the fridge when you are ready to serve and add the club soda. Add ice to 6 wide mouthed wine glasses and pour the Spanish Orange Kush Sangria over the ice to serve.

Product Yield

This recipe for Spanish Orange Kush Sangria produces 6 servings. Dose strength per serving will be determined by what you choose from the dosing chart.
This Sangria, after the initial overnight process, without club soda can be kept refrigerated for up to 2 days in a covered container.

Indian Shiva Skunk Chicken Curry

Chicken curry is a common dish served all over India, and the selection of spices in the curry will vary between regions. Shiva Skunk lends a spicy flavor with strong Skunk notes, which enhance the aromatics and spices of the dish. This is a great dish to be served when you are in need of the comforting and warming effects of a hot meal.

Directions

Coarsely chop the onion then place in a paella pan with the Shiva Skunk Raw Coconut Oil, sweet potato, cashews, sugar, garlic, spices and herbs. Sauté on medium high for 5 minutes then add the tomato paste and 1 cup water. Stir the tomato paste until fully dissolved in the water. Chop the chicken breasts up then

Mise en place

2 chicken breasts

2 cloves minced garlic

1 onion

1 small can of tomato paste

1 cup water

½ cup raw cashews

½ cup raisins

¼ cup chopped cooked sweet potato

¼ cup crumbled goat cheese to garnish

4 tablespoons Shiva Skunk Raw
   Coconut Oil*

3 tablespoons curry powder

1 tablespoon turbinado sugar

1 teaspoon coriander

1 teaspoon cinnamon

1 teaspoon paprika

1 teaspoon cumin

1 teaspoon ginger

½ teaspoon cayenne pepper

Sea salt and pepper to taste

* Follow the recipe for Raw Coconut Oil on page 39 and add the desired dose of Shiva Skunk or alternative strain by referring to the dosing chart on page 15.

Dietary Lifestyle

O

add to the pan along with the raisins. Cover and simmer for 25 to 30 minutes on low or until the sauce thickens.

Season the curry with sea salt and pepper then garnish with crumbled goat cheese. Serve over jasmine rice, with oven naan bread or by itself.

Product Yield

This recipe for Indian Shiva Skunk Chicken Curry produces 4 servings. Dose strength per serving will be determined by what you choose from the dosing chart.

Dinner

German Super Nova Meatloaf

In Germany after World War II, meat was scarce, the economy was in ruins, and any roast meat that was for sale was over priced. If families wanted to make a prized roast like rabbit for a special occasion dinner it could prove to be difficult or out of their budget. During this time a meatloaf known as "Falscher Hase" or "false rabbit" became popular as housewives bought the only meat they could afford and molded it into the shape of a rabbit. The strong pine tones and slight bitterness of the Super Nova really balance the heavy, fatty flavors of the meatloaf. Enjoy for a special occasion dinner or during the cool nights of fall or winter for a hearty meal.

Directions

Place the ground beef in a large bowl then add the roughly chopped onion. Pour in the breadcrumbs then all the spices, herbs, sea salt and pepper. Break 2 whole eggs

Mise en place

1 pound ground beef

8 slices raw bacon

8 servings of dosed ground Super Nova*

2 eggs

2 hardboiled eggs

1 sweet onion

1 cup beef stock plus 1 cup reserve

½ cup breadcrumbs

¼ cup tomato paste

3 tablespoons flour

1 tablespoon parsley

1 tablespoon rosemary

1 teaspoon paprika

½ teaspoon sea salt

½ teaspoon black pepper

* Add the desired dose of Super Nova or alternative strain by referring to the dosing chart on page 15.

Dietary Lifestyle

O

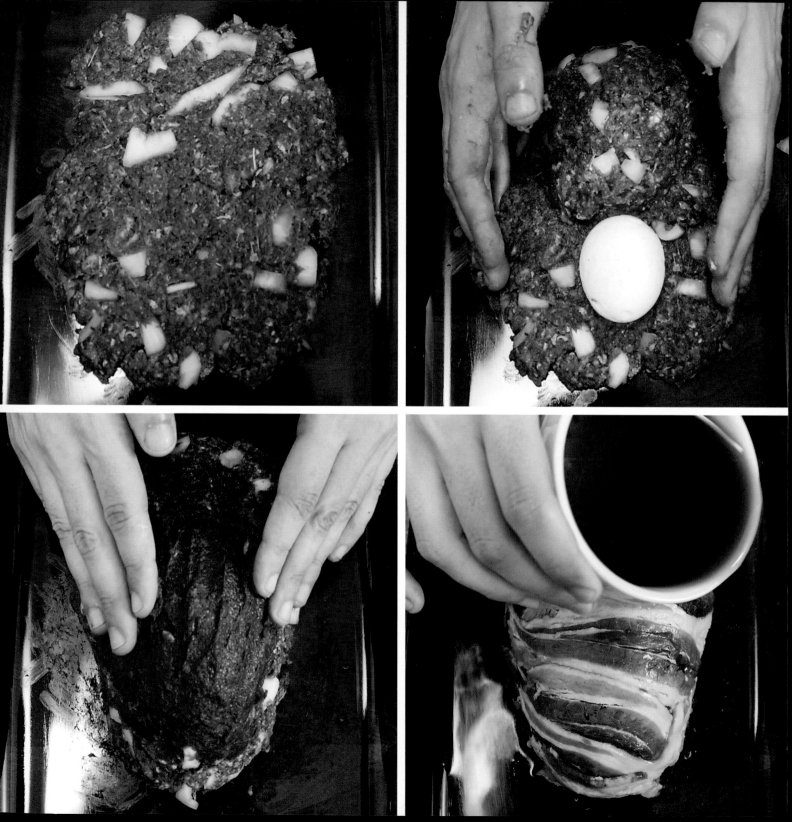

into the bowl as well as the ground Super Nova. Mix all of these ingredients with your hands until well incorporated.

Spread ½ this mixture into a baking dish then place 2 hard-boiled eggs evenly on top of the meat mixture. Take the other ½ of the meat mixture and mold it around the eggs while making sure all gaps are sealed. Spread the tomato paste on top of the meatloaf then wrap the bacon around the top and sides of the loaf. Pour the beef stock over the meatloaf then sprinkle the flour into the beef broth.

Cover with tinfoil and bake at 375°F for 1 hour. If the beef broth level runs low make sure to add more from your reserve. After the baking time is done, let the meatloaf rest for 10 minutes before slicing to serve. If desired, you may pour the reduced stock over your meatloaf.

Product Yield

This recipe for German Super Nova Meatloaf creates 8 servings. Your dose per serving will depend on the medication strength you pick from the dosing chart.

The Catalan Conquistador Steak

The region of Catalonia in northeastern Spain has a very rich form of cuisine that relies heavily on seasonal items grown along the Mediterranean coast. Dishes are vibrant and fresh, reflecting the changing seasons. The Conquistador strain has a very strong, sweet, citrus flavor that really makes the topping of this steak pop with freshness. This is a great dish to enjoy whenever you are in need of a zesty and luscious T-bone steak.

Directions

Season the T-bone steak with sea salt and peppercorns. Chop the tomato and place in a medium sized bowl. Add the chopped basil, garlic, ½ tablespoon non-medicated olive oil, and sliced peel mixture. When slicing the peel make sure to

Mise en place

1 large T-bone steak

1 tomato

1 clove minced garlic

¼ cup thinly sliced orange and lemon peel or zest mix

1 tablespoon chopped basil

1 tablespoon non-medicated olive oil

1 tablespoon Clarified Herbed Conquistador Cannabutter*

Sea salt and peppercorns to season

* Follow the recipe for Clarified Herbed Cannabutter on page 29 and add the desired dose of Conquistador or alternative strain by referring to the dosing chart on page 15.

Dietary Lifestyle

O, GF

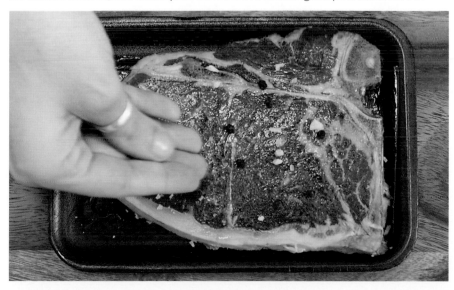

trim the pith or white part of the rind. If this is a texture you do not enjoy, simply zest the orange and lemon instead. Stir this topping mixture with a spoon then cover and set aside so the flavors to deepen.

Pour the remaining ½ tablespoon non-medicated olive oil into a frying pan and set it over a medium high heat. Add the steak and cook for 4 minutes on each side. Plate the steak and rub 1 tablespoon Clarified Herbed Conquistador Cannabutter over the top. Now uncover the topping mixture and spoon on top of the T-bone steak to serve.

Product Yield

This recipe for The Catalan Conquistador Steak produces 1 serving but can be doubled, tripled, quadrupled, etc., to fit the amount of servings required. Your dose per serving will depend on the medication strength you pick from the dosing chart.

American Tex-Mex Herijuana Cinnamon Chili

Mise en place

Chili, contrary to popular belief, was not developed in Mexico but rather in America as trail food. Originally it consisted of dried beef, beef fat, dried chili peppers and salt. This mixture was then dried and packaged so that it could be stored for long periods of time before being dissolved into a boiling pot of water for consumption. It wasn't until many years later that beans found their way into the dish. The deep hashy flavors of Herijuana add a complexity and richness to this dish that will have you licking your spoon with each bite. This is a great dish to be enjoyed on a cool evening when you are in need of a satisfied belly.

Directions

Coarsely chop the mini assorted sweet peppers, sweet onion and garlic then place in a stockpot with 1 tablespoon non-medicated olive oil. Sauté the vegetables then add the ground bison and cook for 5 minutes over a high heat, stirring often.

Turn the heat to medium low and add the kidney beans, pinto beans, crushed fire roasted tomatoes and 3 tablespoons of non-medicated olive oil into the

10 mini assorted sweet peppers
6 servings of dosed ground Herijuana*
4 garlic cloves
4 tablespoons non-medicated olive oil
1 pound ground bison
1 can crushed fire roasted tomatoes
1 can small tomato paste
1 can kidney beans
1 can pinto beans
1 large sweet onion
¼ cup turbinado sugar
2 teaspoons paprika
2 teaspoons chili powder
2 teaspoons Mexican ancho chili
   powder
2 teaspoons cinnamon
1 ½ cinnamon sticks
1 teaspoon allspice
½ teaspoon cayenne pepper

* Add the desired dose of Herijuana or alternative strain by referring to the dosing chart on page 15.

Dietary Lifestyle

O, GF

stockpot. Then add in your tomato paste making sure to scrape the entire can. Take this can and fill it up twice with water and add to the pot. Stir all of these ingredients together until they are well incorporated. Pour the ground up cannabis into the mixture and stir. Finally, add the spices followed by the sugar and give your mixture a few good stirs.

Cover your stockpot with a lid and set the temperature to low and let the chili simmer for 60 minutes. Serve in a bowl garnished with cheese and use crackers or fresh bread to dip into the chili.

Product Yield

This recipe for American Tex-Mex Herijuana Cinnamon Chili produces 6 servings. Your dose per serving will depend on the medication strength you pick from the dosing chart.

Hungarian Wappa Goulash

Goulash is a popular dish that was originally made by cattle herders in Hungarian cuisine. Hungarian stews do not rely on the thickening agents of flour but rather the starch from the potatoes. The pungent, earthy and musky yet somewhat fruity Wappa strain was born to intermingle with all the ingredients of this dish. Enjoy this dish when you are in need of a nourishing stew that will warm the soul.

Directions

Coarsely chop the onions and place inside a large stew pot with 4 tablespoons Basic Clarified Wappa Cannabutter. Cook over a medium heat until translucent, then add in the cubed stew meat. Let the stew meat cook till just rare then add in the sliced carrot, chopped potatoes, tomato and parsnip.

Pour 3 cups of water into the stew pot followed by the paprika, marjoram, caraway seeds and sliced garlic. Stir this mixture on medium for 1 minute then add 1 small can of tomato paste. Gently mix the tomato paste until fully combined and

Mise en place

1 pound cubed stew meat

3 cups water

2 small potatoes

2 sweet onions

1 small can tomato paste

1 large carrot

1 large parsnip

1 tomato

1 large clove garlic

4 tablespoons Basic Clarified Wappa
  Cannabutter*

4 tablespoons paprika

2 tablespoons marjoram

2 tablespoons caraway seeds

Sea salt and pepper to taste

* Follow the recipe for Basic Clarified Cannabutter on page 27 and add the desired dose of Wappa or alternative strain by referring to the dosing chart on page 15.

Dietary Lifestyle

O, GF

dissolved in the water. Cover the stew pot and reduce the temperature to low then simmer for 1 hour.

When your Hungarian Wappa Goulash is ready, season with sea salt and pepper to taste then serve in a bowl paired with rye bread.

Product Yield

This recipe for Hungarian Wappa Goulash produces 4 large servings. Dose strength per serving will be determined by what you choose from the dosing chart.

Dinner

Sicilian Somativa Veal Marsala

Marsala is a seaport city in the west section of Sicily where the fortified wine "Marsala" was born. This wine was originally fortified with brandy so that it would make the wine last longer during the long ocean journeys. Many delicious dishes were created using Marsala wine. The sweet Skunk and floral pine taste of Somativa marry with the flavors of the Marsala wine creating an exceptional taste. When you are in the mood for a little taste of Sicily, this is the perfect dish to delight in.

Directions

Slice the veal evenly into 4 servings or into smaller scaloppini style cuts. If you cut the meat scaloppini style, make sure to divide the meat evenly per dish. Sift the flour into a medium sized bowl then dredge the veal cuts in the flour. Add the non-medicated olive oil to a frying pan and bring the heat up to medium high. Season the veal with sea salt and pepper then add to the pan. Cook for 2 minutes on each side then pull from the pan and place onto a baking sheet. Cover the baking sheet with tinfoil and place into the oven on warm. This will keep the veal

Mise en place

1 pound veal

1 carton sliced mushrooms

1 cup beef stock

2 cloves garlic minced

⅔ cup sweet marsala wine

⅓ cup all-purpose flour plus 1
    tablespoon reserve

4 tablespoons Basic Clarified
    Somativa Cannabutter*

3 tablespoons non-medicated olive oil

1 teaspoon thyme

1 teaspoon oregano

Sea salt and pepper to taste

* Follow the recipe for Basic Clarified Cannabutter on page 27 and add the desired dose of Somativa or alternative strain by referring to the dosing chart on page 15.

Dietary Lifestyle

O

Dinner

from turning cold. Do not turn the oven up past warm or your veal will overcook.

Deglaze the pan by adding the marsala wine and scraping the bottom of the pan with a spatula. Now add the garlic, thyme, oregano, Basic Clarified Somativa Cannabutter, sliced mushrooms and beef stock. Cook the sauce mixture on medium for 5 minutes then add 1 tablespoon reserved all-purpose flour. Stir in the flour then cook for 5 to 8 minutes or until the sauce reduces and thickens.

Pull the veal from the oven and plate. Divide the sauce into 4 servings and spoon over the plated veal. Garnish with fresh herbs and serve.

Product Yield

This recipe for Sicilian Somativa Veal Marsala produces 4 servings. Dose strength per serving will be determined by what you choose from the dosing chart.

French Chrystal Salmon en Papillote

The French term "en papillote" means "in parchment," which is a method used in French cuisine where a food item is placed into sealed parchment paper then baked. Generally, this method of cooking is reserved for fish or chicken. The heavy citrus and kerosene-like attributes from the strain Chrystal impart a complex citrus flavor into the salmon. Enjoy this dish with a fine glass of White Bordeaux or Pouilly Fumé.

Directions

Take a large sheet of parchment paper and fold in half. Lay the folded sheet of parchment paper so that the folded edge is to your left. With a non-toxic marker draw half a heart starting at the top where the fold starts and end where the

Mise en place

Parchment paper cut into the shape of a heart

1 salmon boned filet (4 to 6 ounces)

2 slices orange

2 slices lemon

2 sprigs dill

1 tablespoon Clarified Herbed Cannabutter*

Sea Salt and peppercorns to season

* Follow the recipe for Clarified Herbed Cannabutter on page 29 and add the desired dose of Chrystal or alternative strain by referring to the dosing chart on page 15.

Dietary Lifestyle

O, P, GF

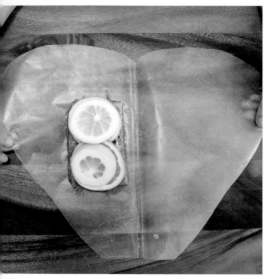

bottom of the fold is. Follow the non-toxic marker line with scissors then unfold to reveal a heart. Trim the bottom of the heart so that it is flat.

Add the salmon filet to the center of one side of the heart. Sprinkle the peppercorns on top of the salmon filet. Lay the dill sprigs on top of the salmon to make sure they fit the length of the filet then remove. Spread the Clarified Herbed Chrystal Cannabutter on top of the salmon filet and peppercorns. Season with sea salt then lay the dill sprigs, orange slices and lemon slices on top. Fold the heart over and, starting at the flat end of the heart, roll the edges up with your fingers until you reach the other end. Place into a baking dish and bake at 375°F for 12 minutes.

Pull from the oven then plate while warm. Cut open the middle of the parchment paper right after the plate has been served. This will allow the steam and aromas to hit the nose of the person eating the dish.

Product Yield

This recipe for French Chrystal Salmon en Papillote produces 1 serving but can be doubled, tripled, quadrupled, etc., to fit the amount of servings required. Your dose per serving will depend on the medication strength you pick from the dosing chart.

Dinner

Russian Sputnik Beef Stroganoff

Beef stroganoff is dish that's often served up in Russia, and it was developed in the 19th century. It was so popular that it spread to neighboring countries and even to other parts of the world. Sputnik adds a great amount of creaminess and richness to the sauce. Partake in this during the cool fall months or cold winter months when energy and warmth is needed.

Directions

In a large stew pot over a medium heat, place 4 tablespoons of Basic Clarified Sputnik Cannabutter or non-medicated butter, onion, mushrooms and garlic. Sauté this mixture until the onions become translucent then add in the cubed stew meat and cook until about medium rare.

Turn the heat to medium low then add the cream, dosed ground decarboxylated Russian Sputnik** if you chose not to add in the cannabutter, and flour into the

Mise en place

1 pound cubed stew meat

1 small carton mushrooms

1 sweet onion chopped

2 cloves minced garlic

1 ½ cup heavy cream

¾ cup sour cream

⅓ cup flour

4 tablespoons Basic Clarified Sputnik Cannabutter or non-medicated butter*

4 servings of dosed ground decarboxylated Russian Sputnik**

4 servings of cooked egg noodles

Sea salt and pepper to taste

* Follow the recipe for Basic Clarified Cannabutter on page 27 and add the desired dose of Sputnik or alternative strain by referring to the dosing chart on page 16.
**Add the desired dose of decarboxylated Russian Sputnik or alternative strain by referring to the dosing chart on page 15 if you choose not to use the Basic Clarified Sputnik Cannabutter.

Dietary Lifestyle

O

Dinner

pot. Stir this mixture to make sure all ingredients are fully incorporated. Drop the heat to low and let this mixture cook for 15 minutes.

While your sauce is cooking boil up 4 servings of egg noodles and make sure to time it up for when the sauce is ready. When the sauce has thickened stir in the sour cream and heat to warm only. Season with sea salt and pepper and then pour over plated egg noodles.

Product Yield

This recipe for Russian Sputnik Stroganoff produces 4 servings. Dose strength per serving will be determined by what you choose from the dosing chart.

Italian Eggplant In Red Devil Sauce

Eggplant is a common vegetable used in numerous Italian dishes throughout the various regions. Dishes range from very complex to very simplistic but all are delicious. This specific recipe for baked eggplant is a rustic style dish that is perfect for any family affair. The heavy floral and forest flavors of the Red Devil strain bring out the flavors of the eggplant, sauce, mushrooms and seasonings. Enjoy family style with your loved ones or by yourself when you wish to medicate with some Italian style.

Directions

Roughly chop the onion and sauté in a pan with 2 tablespoons non-medicated olive oil until translucent. Then add the sliced mushrooms and dosed ground Red Devil. Sauté this mixture until the mushrooms reduce in volume then add the minced garlic, Italian seasoning and fennel. After adding the spices sauté for a few more minutes then pull from the stove to cool.

Pour the tomato puree, red wine plus 1½ cups water into a saucepan and stir the

Mise en place

8 servings of dosed ground Red Devil*

2 cloves minced garlic

2 large sprigs of fresh basil

1 large eggplant

1 small carton of sliced mushrooms

1 can tomato paste

1 onion

1 cup shredded mozzarella cheese

¼ cup red wine

¼ cup shredded Parmesan cheese

3 tablespoons non-medicated olive oil

1 tablespoon Italian seasoning

1 teaspoon fennel

Sea salt and pepper

* Add the desired dose of Red Devil or alternative strain by referring to the dosing chart on page 15.

Dietary Lifestyle

O, OLV, LV, P

mixture together over a low heat for 5 minutes. Pull from the stove and set aside.

Spoon the entire onion and mushroom mixture into the bottom of a 3 quart baking dish evenly. Spread ½ of the sauce mixture and sprinkle ½ the shredded mozzarella cheese over the onion and mushroom mixture. Now lay the sliced eggplant down evenly, allowing for overlapping. Spoon the remaining sauce and sprinkle the remaining cheese over the eggplant slices. Season with sea salt and pepper then cover the baking dish with tinfoil. Bake in a preheated 375 degree oven for 55 minutes. After the 55 minutes is up, remove the tinfoil and sprinkle ¼ cup shredded Parmesan cheese over the Italian Eggplant in Red Devil Sauce. Bake for another 5 minutes then pull from the oven, garnish with the fresh basil and serve.

Product Yield

This recipe for Italian Eggplant in Red Devil Sauce produces 8 servings. Your dose per serving will depend on the medication strength you pick from the dosing chart.

Dinner

Moroccan Mazar Lamb

Mise en place

Lamb is a common meat used in Moroccan cuisine, and in this dish it is flavored with an intricate array of spices and herbs. Most lamb is either cooked in a tajine, over the fire, stewed in a pot or baked into a pastilla. The robust sandalwood and pine flavors of Mazar deepen and ripen the taste of the sauce. Whenever you are in need of an authentic spicy taste of Morocco this is the dish for you.

Directions

Coarsely chop the onion and add it to a stockpot with the 4 tablespoons Basic Clarified Mazar Cannbutter. Add all of the spices, herbs and garlic then sauté on medium until the onions have reduced in size. Debone lamb shoulder then cut into cubes. Add the cubed lamb into the stockpot and sauté until browned.

Chop up the tomato then add to the stockpot with the tomato paste and water. Stir

- 1 pound lamb shoulder chops
- 2 cloves minced garlic
- 1 white onion
- 1 tomato
- 2 cups water
- ½ small can tomato paste
- 4 tablespoons Basic Clarified Mazar Cannbutter*
- 1 tablespoon paprika
- 1 tablespoon cumin
- 1 tablespoon cinnamon
- 1 tablespoon turmeric
- 1 tablespoon ginger
- ½ teaspoon cayenne pepper
- ½ teaspoon cardamom
- Sea salt and pepper

* Follow the recipe for Basic Clarified Cannabutter on page 27 and add the desired dose of Mazar or alternative strain by referring to the dosing chart on page 15.

Dietary Lifestyle

O, GF (do not serve over couscous for GF)

this mixture then cover with a lid. Turn the heat down to low and simmer for 1 hour. Season with sea salt and pepper then serve over couscous.

Product Yield

This recipe for Moroccan Mazar Lamb produces 4 servings. Dose strength per serving will be determined by what you choose from the dosing chart.

SECTION SEVEN

Desserts

Indian Kalichakra Sweet Carrot Pudding

French Mixed Berry Kush Compote

American Chocolope Frosted Raw Brownies

American Somalicious Kief Applesauce

Egyptian Nebula Semolina Cake

American Chewy Vegan Chocolate Thai
Kief Chip Cookies

Japanese Green Tea Mochi Ice Cream

The American Romulan Ho Ho Cupcake

American ABV Strawberry Shortcake

German Vanilla Kush Marzipan

Indian Kalichakra Sweet Carrot Pudding

Indian sweet carrot pudding, also known as "gajar halwa" or "Gajar Ka Halwa" is an immensely popular dessert dish in India. This dish will often be served at traditional Indian wedding banquets or during Diwali festival celebrations. The sweet, fruity and slightly minty flavoring of Kalichakra melds with the cardamom and sweetened condensed milk. This is a nutritious, delicately sweet and delightful dessert that won't result in any form of "dessert guilt" afterwards.

Directions

Place the Basic Clarified Kalichakra Cannabutter, raisins and cashews into a frying pan. Sauté this mixture on medium high for 3 minutes while constantly stirring. Immediately reduce the heat to medium and add in the shredded carrots. Add in the milk and condensed milk, and simmer this mixture on medium for 10 minutes while stirring occasionally to break up any clumps.

After 10 minutes of simmering, stir in the sugar and continue to cook this mixture on the same setting until the liquid is absorbed by the carrots. This process will take

Mise en place

5 large carrots shredded

1 cup milk

½ cup sweetened condensed milk

½ cup turbinado sugar

½ cup raisins

¼ cup raw cashews

4 tablespoons Basic Clarified
    Kalichakra Cannabutter*

1 teaspoon cardamom powder

*Follow the recipe for Basic Clarified Cannabutter on page 27 and add the desired dose of Kalichakra or alternative strain by referring to the dosing chart on page 15.

Dietary Lifestyle

O, OLV, LV, P, GF

approximately 15 minutes. Make sure you stir the mixture while it cooks to prevent the mixture from over-caramelizing. After the liquid is absorbed, pull from heat and stir in the cardamom powder.

Serve this dessert warm from the pan with vanilla ice cream on top or serve it chilled by itself. You can serve it as shown in the picture by pouring the mixture into a small bowl or large ramekin and allowing it to cool and set to that shape, then turning it out onto a plate. Indian Kalichakra Sweet Carrot Pudding can be stored in the refrigerator for up to 1 week.

Product Yield

This recipe for Kalichakra Indian Sweet Carrot Pudding produces 4 servings at ½ cup each. Dose strength per serving will be determined by what you choose from the dosing chart.

French Mixed Berry Kush Compote

The French term "compote" translates to "mixture," and is a dessert that originated in the 17th century. The sweet blueberry and berry profiles of Berry Kush make this the perfect strain to escalate the berry flavors in this dish. Serve this dish warm by itself or accompanied with ice cream, or cold with a dollop of fresh whipped cream for a refreshing berry delight.

Directions

Place the sugar, vanilla extract and water into a stockpot then stir until fully dissolved. Slice the strawberries then add them to the pot with whole

Mise en place

3 cups mixed berries (strawberries, blackberries and blueberries)

4 tablespoons Compound Strawberry Berry Kush Honey Cannabutter*

¼ cup turbinado sugar

¼ cup water

Zest from 1 lemon

2 teaspoons vanilla extract

1½ teaspoons cornstarch

1 teaspoon cinnamon

*Follow the recipe for Compound Strawberry Honey Cannabutter on page 31 and add the desired dose of Berry Kush or alternative strain by referring to the dosing chart on page 15.

Dietary Lifestyle

O, OLV, OV, LV, P, GF

Desserts

blackberries and blueberries. Add the Compound Strawberry Berry Kush Honey Cannabutter, lemon zest and cinnamon.

Bring this berry mixture to a boil then sprinkle in the cornstarch and gently stir until fully dissolved. Let the berry mixture boil for about 1 to 2 minutes then quickly reduce the heat to low and let it simmer for another 5 minutes. You can serve the French Mixed Berry Kush Compote warm or cold.

Product Yield

This recipe for French Mixed Berry Kush Compote produces 4 servings. Dose strength per serving will be determined by what you choose from the dosing chart.

American Chocolope Frosted Raw Brownies

Brownies were originally introduced into the dessert world in the United States in the late 19th century. They rose to popularity because of they were a tasty hybrid between a cake and a cookie. I wanted to create a recipe to reflect the popularity of the raw foods movement in the United States; one that tasted like a brownie but was a healthier option. Chocolope lends a deep chocolate flavor with hints of sweet fruit and a faint smokiness that makes these brownies taste like the real deal. Sit back and relax while enjoying these brownies with either a big glass of milk, coconut milk, coffee or even tea.

Directions

Place the mixed nuts, rolled dates, cocoa powder, flax seeds, non-medicated raw coconut oil, honey, vanilla extract, almond extract and sea salt in a food processor. Process this mixture until it is well combined and creates a very moist crumbly

Mise en place

Raw brownies

1 cup of mixed walnuts, pecans and hazelnuts

1 cup rolled dates in coconut flakes*

¼ cup cocoa powder

¼ cup flax seeds**

4 tablespoons non-medicated raw coconut oil

1 teaspoon raw honey or clover honey

1½ teaspoons vanilla extract

1 teaspoon almond extract

1 pinch crushed sea salt

* Or 1 cup chopped dates combined with ¼ cup chopped coconut flakes
** You can use flax seed meal instead of seeds for a chewier softer brownie. If you want a nuttier brownie keep the flax seeds in their shells. Either way will be equally delicious!

Dietary Lifestyle

O, OLV, OV, LV, P, GF

Desserts

mixture. Spread this mixture evenly into an 8 x 8 square pan and then press the mixture into the pan with a flat hand. Keep pressing with a flat hand until the mixture compresses evenly.

In a separate bowl, combine the Chocolate Raw Coconut Oil, agave nectar, cocoa powder and vanilla extract. Whip with a spoon or whisk until the frosting comes together and becomes uniform in texture. After about 5 minutes of whipping your frosting by hand, pour it directly onto the pan mixture and smooth it out evenly with a spoon. Put the pan into the fridge and let it set for 1 hour. Pull from the fridge after your time is up and score into 8 brownies with a knife. Store your raw brownies in a container in the refrigerator for up to 1 week.

Product Yield

This recipe for American Chocolope Frosted Raw Brownies will produce 8 servings. Your dose per serving will depend on the medication strength you pick from the dosing chart.

Mise en place

Raw frosting

½ cup Chocolope Raw Coconut Oil***

¼ cup agave nectar

¼ cup cocoa powder

1 teaspoon vanilla extract

***Follow the recipe for Raw Coconut Oil on page 39 and add the desired dose of Chocolope or alternative strain by referring to the dosing chart on page 15.

American Somalicious Kief Applesauce

Applesauce was created by cooks in Medieval Europe to act as an accompaniment to a variety of foods. This tradition was later taken to America by settlers and applesauce was traditionally prepared during late fall or right before winter. The heavy hash and sweet notes of Somalicious bring about a taste reminiscent of fall time treats. Enjoy this dish either warm or cold with lightly sprinkled cinnamon on top.

Directions

Wash and peel the apples then cut into chunky pieces with a small paring knife. Place the apple chunks into a stockpot or paella pan. Then add the water, lemon juice, vanilla extract, brown sugar, cinnamon and decarboxylated Somalicious kief.

Cover with a lid and bring the apple mixture to a boil for 5 minutes then drop to a low heat. Simmer for 30 to 40 minutes or until tender, stirring occasionally. Mash the apples for chunky applesauce or place into a food processor for smooth applesauce. Serve warm or cold.

Product Yield

This recipe for American Somalicious Kief Applesauce produces six servings. Dose strength per serving will be determined by what you choose from the dosing chart.

Mise en place

3 pounds Fuji apples

6 servings of dosed decarboxylated Somalicious kief*

1 cup water

½ cup brown sugar

3 tablespoons lemon juice

2 teaspoons cinnamon

2 teaspoons vanilla extract

* Add the desired dose of decarboxylated Somalicious kief or alternative decarboxylated strain kief into this dish per serving by referring to the dosing chart on page 15 and decarboxylation process on page 16.

Dietary Lifestyle

O, OLV, OV, LV, P, GF

Egyptian Nebula Semolina Cake

Egyptian semolina cake, also known as "basbousa," is a popular dessert that is served in Egypt. Nebula balances the sweetness of this cake with a subtle earthiness and plays off the syrup with its sweet, tangy Skunk undertones. This is the perfect little cake to be served with a dark roast coffee or a black tea when you are in need of a pick-me-up.

Directions for syrup

In a saucepan, bring the water and lemon juice to a boil. Add the sugar to the water mixture and reduce heat to medium for 10 minutes. Remove from the heat then add in the orange extract and rose water. Stir until fully combined and set aside for when the cake comes out of the oven.

Mise en place

Syrup

2 cups turbinado sugar

1½ cups water

2 tablespoons orange extract

2 tablespoons lemon juice

1 tablespoon rose water

*Follow the recipe for Basic Clarified Cannabutter on page 27 and add the desired dose of Nebula or alternative strain by referring to the dosing chart on page 15.

Dietary Lifestyle

O, OLV, LV, P

Directions for the cake

Preheat the oven to 350°F. In a large bowl cream the sugar and Basic Clarified Nebula Cannabutter together. Add one egg at a time and then the vanilla extract, making sure to fully blend all of the ingredients. Stir in the baking powder and

baking soda then alternate between adding the semolina and the yogurt a little at a time, whisking constantly.

Pour the mixture into a greased 9x12 inch pan and bake for 30 to 35 minutes. Remove the cake after it has finished baking and place the pecans on top as shown, so that when the cake is sliced, each piece will have one pecan on the top of it in the middle of the slice. Pour the syrup evenly over the cake. Let the cake soak up the syrup fully and then serve.

Product Yield

This recipe for Egyptian Nebula Semolina Cake will produce 8 servings of cake with 2 slices per serving. Your dose per serving will depend on the medication strength you pick from the dosing chart.

Mise en place

Cake

2 cups semolina

2 eggs

¾ cup plain yogurt

¾ cup turbinado sugar

½ cup Basic Clarified Nebula
 Cannabutter*

½ cup whole raw pecans

1 teaspoon vanilla extract

1 teaspoon baking powder

½ teaspoon baking soda

American Chewy Vegan Chocolate Thai Kief Chip Cookies

Chocolate chip cookies were accidently created by Ruth Graves Wakefield in 1930 when she ran out of baker's chocolate and tried to substitute with semi-sweet chocolate from Nestlé. She decided to sell her recipe to Nestlé in exchange for a lifetime supply of their chocolate chips. Even though this recipe is designed as a vegan recipe it tastes just as good as its non-vegan counterpart. The strong chocolate taste and rich-bodied coffee undertone of Chocolate Thai enhances the richness of the chocolate chips in this cookie. Reward yourself by

Mise en place

Dosed decarboxylated Chocolate Thai Kief*

1¼ cup all-purpose flour

1 cup wheat flour

1 cup vegan margarine

1 heaping cup vegan chocolate chips

½ cup vegan brown sugar

½ cup vegan turbinado sugar

5 tablespoons coconut milk

1 teaspoon vanilla extract

1 teaspoon almond extract

1 teaspoon baking soda

½ teaspoon sea salt

* Add the desired dose of decarboxylated Chocolate Thai kief or alternative decarboxylated kief into this dish per serving by referring to the dosing chart on page 15 and decarboxylation process on page 16.

Dietary Lifestyle
O, OLV, OV, LV, P, V

Desserts

enjoying this cookie with a big, cold glass of coconut milk that will surely take you back to your childhood.

Directions

In a large bowl, mix together the flours, baking soda, sea salt and room temperature margarine. Then add the brown sugar, turbinado sugar, vanilla extract, almond extract, coconut milk, chocolate chips and kief. Stir this mixture with a large spoon until it forms a soft cookie dough.

Preheat your oven to 350°F and pull out a non-stick cookie sheet. Take a heaping tablespoon of the dough. Roll this dough into your hands and place onto the cookie sheet*. Line the cookie sheet with the raw cookies leaving enough room in between each cookie to prevent them from baking into one another. Bake for 8 to 10 minutes or until edges are lightly brown. Transfer to a cooling rack until the cookies cool down then serve.

Product Yield

*This recipe will create 30 small cookies or 15 large American Chewy Vegan Chocolate Thai chip Cookies. Decide which serving size you want before dosing with the kief as this will ensure proper dosage per cookie. Make sure all ingredients that you use are clearly labeled as being vegan. Your dose per serving will depend on the medication strength you pick from the dosing chart.

Japanese Green Tea Mochi Ice Cream

Japanese Mochi Ice Cream is a confection that was created in 1981 by the company Lotte. Mochi is a glutinous rice cake that is traditionally eaten during a ceremony called mochitsuki, during the New Year and even year round. Mochi ice cream was based on the dessert "daifuku" which was mochi stuffed with a sweetened red bean paste. The sugary vanilla tones of the strain Ice Cream adds an extra depth of creaminess to the green tea ice cream filling. This dessert is the perfect end to a sushi meal or even enjoyed alone when you are in the mood for unusual ice cream.

Directions

Place the Japanese glutinous rice flour, sugar and salt together in a medium microwaveable bowl. In another bowl, scoop out the green tea ice cream and stir with a spoon until it reaches a soft serve state. You can choose to add 6 servings of dosed decarboxylated Ice Cream kief* into either the mochi dough or green tea ice

Mise en place

2 cups Japanese glutinous rice flour (mochiko)

6 servings of dosed decarboxylated Ice Cream kief*

3 cups green tea ice cream

3 cups water

3 teaspoons sugar

1 teaspoon salt

* Add the desired dose of decarboxylated Ice Cream kief or alternative decarboxylated kief into this dish per serving by referring to the dosing chart on page 15 and decarboxylation process on page 16.

Dietary Lifestyle

O, OLV, LV, P, GF (make sure ice cream has no fillers and is labeled GF)

cream centre. When you've done this, put the green tea ice cream into the freezer to set or about 5 minutes.

Add 3 cups of water to your dry mix ingredients then stir with your hands until fully combined. Cover, then place into the microwave for 8 to 10 minutes or until all water is absorbed. While your dough is microwaving, pull the green tea ice cream from the freezer when set and scoop into 6 ice cream balls that equal ½ cup each. Place into the freezer for 10 minutes or until the ice cream balls are firm to the touch.

Turn the mochi dough onto rice-floured or lightly corn-starched board. Knead the dough then roll out and cut 6 large circles from it. Gently roll each circle out into a thin circular sheet of dough. Take 1 rolled out circle and then 1 green tea ice cream ball out of the freezer. Place the green tea ice cream ball in the center and fold the dough over. Bring up one end of the rolled dough and gently press into the middle. Then bring up the other end of the dough and gently press to close. Repeat. As you create your Japanese Green Tea Mochi Ice Cream, place them onto a chilled sheet pan and place into the freezer covered as you go along.

When you are ready to serve, pull the Japanese Green Tea Mochi Ice Cream out of the freezer and let it thaw for a few minutes before serving, but not too much that it melts all over the serving dish or plate.

Product Yield

This recipe for Japanese Green Tea Mochi Ice Cream produces 6 servings. Dose strength per serving will be determined by what you choose from the dosing chart.

Desserts

The American Romulan Ho Ho Cupcake

The origin of the cupcake is unknown, although the first mention of it in text can be found in the cookbook "American Cookery" from 1796. Cupcakes come in various sizes and flavor combinations that are delightful to both children and adults alike. The pungently sweet Romulan strain, which also has spicy tones, pairs so well with the richness of the chocolate cake and ganache topping. This little cake is a decadent and rich way to satisfy a chocolate or sweet tooth craving.

Directions

Place the sugar and room temperature butter into a large mixing bowl and stir together. Add the vanilla extract, almond extract, half of the flour, cocoa powder, baking powder, baking soda, sea salt and 2 eggs. Then add the rest of the flour followed by the milk then stir or whisk until the batter becomes smooth and

Mise en place

20 servings of dosed ground decarboxylated Romulan *

2 eggs

1 extra large piping bag full of heavy whipped cream or vanilla buttercream

1½ cup turbinado sugar

1⅓ cup all-purpose flour

¾ cup cocoa powder

¾ cup milk

3 tablespoons non-medicated room temperature butter

2 teaspoons baking powder

1 teaspoon vanilla extract

1 teaspoon almond extract

¼ teaspoon baking soda

1 pinch sea salt

*Add the desired dose of decarboxylated Romulan or alternative strain by referring to the dosing chart on page 15.

Dietary Lifestyle

O, OLV, P

creamy. Add the dosed ground decarboxylated Romulan then fold the cake batter until evenly distributed.

Line a cupcake tray with cupcake papers and preheat your oven to 350°F. Fill each cupcake liner ⅔ of the way full then place into the oven to bake for 15 to 18 minutes or until a toothpick comes out clean.

Cool the cupcakes completely on a wire rack then pipe either heavy whipped cream or vanilla buttercream into each cupcake. If you want a light airy cupcake use the heavy whipped cream to fill the center of the cupcakes, but if you want a dense luscious center use the vanilla buttercream for your cupcakes. Start by pressing the piping tip into the middle of the cake from the top and slowly pressing the piping bag. Allow the filling to slightly expand the cupcake but stop before the cupcake filling blows out. Place all filled cupcakes on a rack and set aside until your ganache is done.

Place the chocolate chips in metal bowl while bringing the heavy cream to a boil in a saucepan. Once the cream comes to a boil pour over the chocolate chips and whisk or stir until the ganache sauce forms. Dip each cupcake top into the ganache and then set back onto the wire rack to set. Plate and serve.

Product Yield

This recipe for The American Romulan Ho Ho Cupcake produces 20 cupcakes or servings. Dose strength per serving will be determined by what you choose from the dosing chart.

Mise en place
Ganache Icing
1 bag semi-sweet chocolate chips
1 cup heavy cream

American ABV Strawberry Shortcake

Although the origin of this shortcake is unknown, food historians do know that shortcakes were initially invented in Europe in the late 1500's. The earliest recipe for strawberry shortcake was published in 1847 in America and it has been a classic dessert since. ABV (already been vaped) cannabis gives the shortcake a light syrupy sweetness with floral tones which pair perfectly with the strawberries. This is a great dish to be served during the summer months for a deliciously light and refreshing dessert.

Directions

Place the flour, the turbinado sugar, baking powder, sea salt, and dosed ABV cannabis into a bowl. Rub the cold butter with your fingers into this mixture until

Mise en place

- 8 servings of dosed ABV cannabis*
- 1 egg
- 1½ cup all-purpose flour
- ½ cup buttermilk plus ¼ reserve
- 3 tablespoons turbinado sugar
- 3 tablespoons cold non-medicated butter
- 1½ teaspoon baking powder
- 1 teaspoon almond extract
- 1 teaspoon lemon extract
- ½ teaspoon sea salt

* Add the desired dose of the ABV (already been vaped) cannabis by referring to the dosing chart on page 15.

Dietary Lifestyle
O, OLV, P

crumbly. Then add the almond extract, lemon extract, ½ cup buttermilk and 1 egg. Stir this mixture until a sticky dough forms but do not over mix. Roll out onto a floured cutting board and cut out 8 circular rounds from the dough.

Preheat the oven to 375°F and place each round onto a sprayed baking sheet. Gently brush each round with the reserved buttermilk. Bake for 12 to 15 minutes or until lightly golden and firm to the touch.

When the shortcake rounds are done, pull them from the oven and cool completely on a wire rack. In a bowl mix the strawberry slices, sugar, vanilla extract and orange extract. Gently macerate the fruit until some of the juices release then stop. Slice the shortcake rounds through the middle, creating 16 slices, then spread the heavy whipped cream onto the 16 slices evenly. Divide the strawberry mixture into 8 servings and spoon each serving onto the 8 bottom halves of shortcake slices Carefully top each shortcake bottom with its partnered slice to make a complete American ABV Strawberry Shortcake.

Product Yield

This recipe for American ABV Strawberry Shortcake produces 8 servings. Dose strength per serving will be determined by what you choose from the dosing chart.

Mise en place

Strawberry and Cream Filling

2 cups sliced strawberries

2 cups of heavy whipped cream

2 tablespoons turbinado sugar

1 tablespoon vanilla extract

1 tablespoon orange extract

Desserts

German Vanilla Kush Marzipan

The exact origin of this almond paste confection is somewhat debated but it certainly found its way into the cuisine of many cultures. Marizipan is particularly popular in Germany, where it is traditionally made in the north but has also spread to other parts of the country. Marzipan is used in many desserts such as cookies, pastries, candies and cakes. Vanilla Kush enhances the sweetness of the almond paste, which creates a delicious contrast to the semi-sweet chocolate drizzle. Every little bite of this confection will send your taste buds on a sweet ride of almond and chocolate bliss.

Directions

Roll out the German marzipan on a cutting board and then carefully pour the dosed decarboxylated Vanilla Kush kief onto it. Gently envelop the kief with the marzipan and knead like dough until the kief is evenly distributed.

In a double boiler on low, melt your chocolate before you start to portion out your marzipan mixture. Keep the chocolate in the double boiler on the stove on low to keep it in liquid form. Now divide the marzipan mixture into 7 servings at 2 ounces each then roll each serving into a ball with your hands. Place this ball on

Mise en place

14 ounces German marzipan

7 servings of dosed decarboxylated Vanilla Kush kief*

¾ cup semi-sweet chocolate chips

* Add the desired dose of decarboxylated Vanilla Kush kief or alternative decarboxylated strain kief by referring to the dosing chart on page 15 and decarboxylation process on page 16.

Dietary Lifestyle

O, OLV, OV, LV, P, GF (make sure chocolate chips do not have any fillers and is labeled GF)

the cutting board and then use your palm to flatten the marzipan mixture into a cookie shape.

Place your cookies onto a wired rack on top of either a cutting board or covered area to catch the falling chocolate. You may either dip the marzipan straight into the chocolate to fully encase it or drizzle it over each marzipan serving. Let the chocolate set by placing into the fridge for 15 minutes then pull from the fridge to bring to room temperature then serve.

If you choose to encase the marzipan in chocolate it will last longer and will not dry out. Only drizzle the chocolate over the top if you are to serve this dessert immediately otherwise the marzipan will dry out faster.

Product Yield

This recipe for German Vanilla Kush Marzipan produces 7 servings. Dose strength per serving will be determined by what you choose from the dosing chart

Resources

jessicacatalano.com

twitter.com/jessicacatalano

instagram.com/chefjessicacatalano

facebook.com/chefjessicacatalano

tiktok.com/@chefjessicacatalano

NORML.org

medicalmarijuana.procon.org/view.resource.php?resourceID=000881

Grotenhermen, Franjo (2002). "Review of Therapeutic Effects." Cannabis and Cannabinoids: Pharmacology, Toxicology and Therapeutic Potential. New York City: Haworth Press. p. 124. ISBN 978-0-7890-1508-2.

Russo EB (2004). "Clinical endocannabinoid deficiency (CECD): can this concept explain therapeutic benefits of cannabis in migraine, fibromyalgia, irritable bowel syndrome and other treatment-resistant conditions?" Neuro Endocrinology Letters 25 (1–2): 31–9. PMID 15159679.

"In the Matter of Marijuana Rescheduling Petition" (Docket #86-22)." US Department of Justice to the Drug Enforcement Administration. September 6, 1988. pp. 56–57. Retrieved 2011-08-12.

medicalmarijuana.procon.org/view.resource.php?resourceID=000145

Downer EJ, Campbell VA (2010). "Phytocannabinoids, CNS cells and development: A dead issue?" Drug and Alcohol Review 29 (1): 91–98. DOI:10.1111/j.1465-3362.2009.00102.x. PMID 20078688.

Burns TL, Ineck JR (2006). "Cannabinoid analgesia as a potential new therapeutic option in the treatment of chronic pain." The Annals of Pharmacotherapy 40 (2): 251–260. DOI:10.1345/aph.1G217. PMID 16449552.

International Cuisine By Michael F. Nenes - John Wiley & Sons (2008) - Hardback - 864 pages - ISBN 0470052406

On Cooking: A Textbook of Culinary Fundamentals / Edition 4 by Sarah R. Labensky, Alan M. Hause, Steven R. Labensky, Priscilla R. Martel

Special Thanks

I would like to thank the pivotal people who helped with the production of this book.

Green Candy Press, thank you for supporting and bringing my progressive and unorthodox methods of cooking with cannabis into the hands of medical cannabis patients in need.

My Father, Mother, Nikki, Gabby, and Anna: thank you for helping me grow into the woman that I am and for the constant love and support. You all have inspired me in your own unique way. I love you all so incredibly much!

My Colorado family (Alli, Marta, Pat and Erik especially) thank you for everything. I am truly blessed to have such amazing people in my life that love these mountains as much as I do.

Chef Painter, thank you for your constant support through Culinary School. You are a true inspiration and have taught me many things through your passion and talent in cooking. I cannot thank you enough!

– Jessica Catalano

Thanks to everyone who helped make this book become a reality. My friends and family for their support throughout the entire process. Most of all my Mom and Dad, the most amazing, beautiful, wonderful, wise and interesting people I know. Thank you so much.

– Tyler Kittock

About the Author

Jessica Catalano is a professional Cannabis Chef who is classically trained, a cannabis edibles expert, recipe developer, food writer, the pioneer of strain specific cannabis cuisine, author of *The Ganja Kitchen Revolution: The Bible of Cannabis Cuisine* published by Green Candy Press, RYT-200 yoga instructor (restorative yoga and chair yoga certifications), and certified ayurveda specialist. She is a Medical Cannabis and Cannabis Lifestyle advocate who has combined her two loves of food and cannabis into stylish medicated dishes for Medical Cannabis patients. She was born and raised in Buffalo, NY and then headed west to Colorado at 23. Catalano holds three culinary degrees: Pastry Arts, Culinary Arts, and Food Service Management that she earned while living in Colorado. Between her education, experience in the bakery and restaurant industry, impressive cannabis industry working experience, and her knowledge of cannabis, she has been called the "OG Cannabis Chef" by many.

Catalano pioneered strain specific cannabis cuisine for flavor, the first chef in the world to publicly do so, by infusing terpenes into cooking and baking via strain specific recipes to elevate the taste in the edibles she creates. What this means is that she uses specific strains in specific recipes to enhance the flavor profiles of the dishes she constructs. For example, Lemon Kush can be paired with Vietnamese Spring Rolls. By doing this, the Lemon Kush will impart a lemony taste with floral and mint undertones which deepens the flavors in this dish because of the similar taste profiles already present in the ingredients. This also helps patients to understand the importance of terpene flavor profiles in recipes for a more enjoyable experience and how each strain will affect their bodies.

Final Notes

In 2009, she began experimenting with Strain Specific Cooking and Baking and launched a blog in June 2010 to share her recipes with medical marijuana patients. *The Ganja Kitchen Revolution* blog was born and turned into a book shortly after, hitting the market as the first Strain Specific Gourmet Cannabis Cookbook. It has quickly become the authority on strain specific cannabis pairings and a must have in any aspiring cannabis chef's cookbook collection. Today Chef Jessica Catalano still produces free recipes for medical marijuana patients to make in the comfort of their own homes.

Currently, Catalano is the Food Writer for the international *SKUNK Magazine* and former cover girl for Tokin' Female of the Month (*Skunk Magazine* Volume 8, Issue 3). In addition to *SKUNK Magazine*, she writes for *Exhale Magazine* as a cannabis recipe contributor. She also has contributed cannabis recipes to Diane Fornbacher's *LadyBud Magazine*, to the national *Cannabis Now Magazine* from its inception, and served as a Culture writer for *Weedmaps*.

Catalano was also named Stoner Girl of Winter 2015 by the *Stoner Girl's Guide*. She is the former Cannabis Chef at Cultivating Spirits who taught the Cooking with Cannabis Class as well as the Sensational Fusion Private Dinners. She cooked for and co-hosted the first cannabis pairing dinner at the 2015 Aspen X Games with the Cultivating Spirits family. Catalano has cooked for celebrities such as Snoop Dogg in Aspen and has served as a judge for the Denver Hightimes U.S Cannabis Cup in 2012, 2013, 2015, and 2016 for Edibles, Topicals, and CBD products. She is also a former reviewer for Seattle products on "The Proper Cannabis Committee" for A Proper High.

She has appeared on TLC, Munchies VICE, and Al Jazeera. Her work has been mentioned in *Vogue Magazine*, *Vice*, Al Jazeera, Brazil's *Carta Capital Magazine*, Buzzfeed, the Associated Press, *The Guardian*, *Business Insider*, *StarChef's Rising Stars Magazine*, *Culture Magazine*, *Skunk Magazine*, *Cannabis Now Magazine*, *Ladybud Magazine*, *FSR Magazine*, *Denver Westword*, the *Aspen Times*, the *Summit Daily*, the *Cannabist*, the *Stoner Girls Guide*, and many more. She has also done cannabis food writing for *StickyGuide*, *Releaf Magazine*, *Smell the Truth*, *The Nug*, PROHBTD, *Whaxy*, *Stuff Stoners Like*, the *Smoking Bud*, *Starchef's*, *Leafly*, *High Times Magazine*, *VICE*, *MUNCHIES*, Colorado's very own weed-rag *The Daily Doobie*, and many other publications.

As a Medical Cannabis patient herself, she has extensive knowledge since early 1997 for medicinal purposes. She continues to strive for excellence both in cooking, baking and Medical Cannabis knowledge. Her goal is to help as many Medical Cannabis patients as she possibly can creating a better quality of life for them. She explores the health benefits of cooking with cannabis which when balanced with good nutrition and a healthy lifestyle can help promote a longer and more fulfilling life. She is also a passionate yogi and martial artist (Taekwondo), who draws upon inspiration from exploring the Pacific Northwest to fuel creativity in the kitchen and gym. Catalano currently resides in a suburb of Seattle, Washington on a micro farm with her husband, daughter Mary Jane, 10 chickens, Bombay cat Mao, Snowshoe Siamese cat Barry, and her Russian Blue cat Rarity. Her recipes and books are a gift to you. She hopes that they bring you good health, happiness, and a return to nature. Happy cooking and baking!

Index

Index

Index

Index

Index

Index

Index

Index